stupid gone viral

When Science and
Reality Collide

KATHY SCOTT PhD, BRIDGET SARIKAS
AND CHRISTINE BESSLER

RETHINK PRESS

First published in Great Britain in 2020
by Rethink Press (www.rethinkpress.com)

Cover image © Shutterstock | Vandathai

Praise

'Today's disrupted and dynamic workplace demands a more centered style of leadership where an individual's sense of purpose and wellbeing is integral to the performance of the organisation. This is certainly true for leaders but also applies to individuals at all levels as this centeredness is what enables us to effectively navigate our increasingly uncertain and complex environment. This book offers a new organisational model especially powerful for women who want to create a world where personal and professional values, beliefs and behaviours lead to one happy, meaningful and fulfilling life.'
—**Christine Brown-Quinn,** The Female Capitalist®

'The authors take you through every aspect of leadership and press the reset button with current best practice for being an effective leader. For new and those not-so-new-leaders, this is a must read and an introspective inventory of your own style and effectiveness in today's rapidly changing environment. Do yourself the favor of reflecting on the questions at the end of each chapter!'
—**Herb Geary,** MBA, BSN, RN, FACHE, Chief Nursing Officer, Santa Barbara Cottage Health

'Rarely do you find three seasoned healthcare professionals provide such timely and real-life experiences. Kathy, Bridget, and Christine really nailed it in this book. A must read for any leader who is serious about truly making a difference and leading their teams forward in the future.'
    —**Win Howard,** CEO Asante Three Rivers Medical Center

'This book is totally relatable no matter what industry you're in. All the right information in one place to lead you to success with a great humor mixed in. Will be buying this book for all my female colleagues - can't wait to be able to share it with them. Looking forward to connecting with this great group of leaders. Thanks for sharing your experiences and knowledge!'
    —**Tiffany Steffen,** RN, BSN, MBA—HCA Managing Partner

'Using the L3 Fusion Model, this book will serve as your guide to transforming your leadership style so that you can lead others through volatile times. The book uses humor and a "keepin' it real" approach so you're able to relate to the science.'
    —**Sua Wolter,** Senior Director, Process Excellence, Cantel

Contents

Foreword

In this timely and entertaining book, three accomplished women provide a guide to improving leadership that can be applied to business, government, and life. More than the empty words and promises we often hear from today's so-called 'leaders', they present an actual structure for achieving quality leadership; it is called The L3 Fusion Model, which (it turns out) is not a form of lumbar spine surgery. And it is far less painful.

Rather, it is an approach to leadership that takes its essence from two attributes: grace and grit. Grace refers to the respect for, and effective communication with, co-workers and colleagues that is so vital to building a successful organization. Grit refers to the

self-confidence and determination so vital to the successful pursuit of the true collective goal.

An example from my world arises when a jurist
feels strongly about a point of law but finds herself
in the minority when it is time to render an appellate
judgment. She shows grit by not surrendering her
considered views solely to appease her colleagues or
to avoid the need to pen a dissent. But she shows grace
by penning that dissent 'respectfully', as we say—in a
way that refrains from personal attacks or the use of
acerbic prose.

While these principles seem somewhat basic at first
blush, the hard part is up to the individual—that is, not
allowing the grit to nullify the grace, and not allowing
the grace to cripple the grit. It is up to the individual
to achieve this balance, moreover, in organizational
structures which often do not lend themselves to
doing so. In structures which are outdated and are
either resistant to change or simply do not see that
the world in which they operate is changing around
it. It is to learning ways to help us and those organizations break free from outdated ways of operating
that this book is dedicated. It is to helping all of us see
the world and concepts of successful leadership more
clearly that these authors are committed.

So, prepare to reap the benefits of the active intellects
and collective experience (also known as wisdom) of
these three professional women. Prepare to marvel at

how they relate their own life experiences—everything from going on a disastrous first date to dodging trophies hurled by an apoplectic CEO—to the leadership principles they espouse. Prepare to be a better leader and enjoy the ride.

The Honorable Kathleen M. O'Malley
Circuit Judge, United States Court of Appeals for the Federal Circuit

Our Story

Our story begins in 2018, when three women, each hired as a consultant in her own respective field, met on a client engagement. Amid the clutter of faces typical of the first days on a new project, we found each other and immediately bonded—at first through laughter, then knowledge and finally mutual respect. We came to realize that the shared sense of humor and ability to laugh at challenges that first drew us to one another would ultimately be the glue that held us together. This glue not only allowed us to withstand and overcome the many professional challenges we faced, but also led us to where we are today, as co-authors of this book.

As our engagement progressed and we were faced with numerous challenges (the greatest of which was ineffective management), we began discussing the shortfalls we'd seen in healthcare and other industries over the past thirty-plus years. Chief among those challenges were leadership styles that were stale, uninspiring and, quite frankly, unhealthy. It was the same old leadership structures (hierarchical), same old theme (my way or the highway) and same old reaction to change (must be you who needs to change—not me).

We knew it was time for a reset. All of us had operated under these same outdated models for years. We agreed it was our time to take what we'd learned, combine it with our scientific knowledge, and pepper in a healthy (and, at times, irreverent) sense of humor to develop a new leadership model for women (but . . .) that embraced healthy living, leading and learning. Thus, L3 Fusion was created.

L3 Fusion combines the experiences of three women with three unique perspectives and a three-pronged approach to help people maneuver through organizational chaos. When we fuse these elements into one leadership model, an energy that fuels a healthier approach to leadership is created—an approach that's more intentional regarding thoughts and actions. It embraces behaviors and relationships (or lack thereof), working within a team (yes—we help you learn how to row with others) and leading in a system or organization (you, too, can be a leader with a purpose).

Our goal for each of you brave individuals who have entrusted your leadership-reset journey to us is for you to feel energized by a new and exciting way to develop your own path to leadership. It's not complicated. It's relatable—and always fun. For if we don't have a sense of humor about it, work becomes just another four-letter word!

Introduction

We are experiencing a global leadership crisis. This crisis impacts our daily lives as we attempt to navigate through organizations built on a foundation of antiquated leadership thinking and practices. This leadership crisis has many causes and consequences, some understood and some not. But one consequence is clear: living in a crisis day after day comes at a high cost to our personal health and the health of our organizations.

In a crisis, people don't sit back. In a crisis, people get involved! We experiment more boldly. We try things we wouldn't have tried before. We become more vulnerable. We pay closer attention. We use the best evidence available to try new things, and we create new evidence when we fail. Some of our interventions will have a disproportionate impact on the crisis. Like an architectural keystone at the apex of an arch that keeps all the other elements in place, some interventions will make a bigger difference. Science and experience tell us that a keystone of healthy leadership today is harnessing the best thinking and contributions of the many. So how do we make this happen?

We human beings have innate needs that counter our outdated operating assumptions—the need to direct our own lives, learn and create new things and contribute in meaningful ways to meaningful causes, for example. Research on what motivates us as humans indicates that the desire for freedom and choice drive our natural state of health. The perception that we have control is an important component of our happiness (Pink 2011). Freedom—to choose, learn, try new methods, be more self-directed—leads to engagement. It's an intrinsic motivator. And while external control may lead to compliance in the short term, it ultimately leads to a less engaged and less productive workforce.

Our fundamental message is this: freedom leads to more; control leads to less. More freedom to do and be and less control over others leads to healthier people and healthier organizations. *What?* No, we're not proposing a free-for-all, nor are we proposing freedom without boundaries. Rather, the evidence tells us that there are ways to provide leadership, direction and essential controls while also enabling freedom, creativity and choice. These ways, in fact, lead to better results.

This book is a response to the leadership crisis. It describes an evolving model of evidence-based leadership called the L3 Fusion Model. This model acknowledges the importance of honoring ourselves and others while influencing the system to get the desired results. It's a model of healthy engagement that attracts others to contribute their best (grace) and a model of achievement through focus and collective action (grit). Leading with grace requires an attitude of respect and the ability to suspend judgment so that we can learn and understand more deeply. Leading with grit requires courage to act with firmness of mind and spirit in the face of difficulty. These leadership attributes of grit and grace, when combined with a shared purpose, systems thinking and structures that support an action culture, create places where people want to work. In these places, leaders and members are encouraged to engage in things that are inspiring and bigger than themselves (purpose). They have more choice about what they do, with whom they do it and how and when they do it (autonomy). Inquiry is supported and encouraged (learning) along with a willingness to experiment one's way into fresh solutions (innovation).

Changing the way we think, behave and lead is a journey. And sometimes it can be an uncomfortable one. This journey is for those who have had enough of the status quo and want to lead more purposefully, more humanely, more scientifically. Spoiler alert—this journey is not about what others should do. It's about you and what you can do to make a difference, regardless of your circumstances.

During our interviews of women in leadership, we were asked to provide a way for you, our readers, to have a more interactive journey with us and the book. We loved the idea, so we've incorporated many of our own stories and experiences to illustrate key points and principles. These stories are all true, although some of the details have been tweaked to protect the identities of those involved, and many (we're told) are highly entertaining. We also include a self-help section at the end of each chapter—a place for you to reflect on your learnings, apply the concepts to your personal experience and jot down any questions you may have. Our hope is that by the time you've read the last chapter and completed your final exercise, you'll be ready to lead more purposefully and feel prepared to do it with joy and laughter!

1
Wake Up!
Preparing To Thrive

Have you ever walked into a room and wanted to yell "Wake up, people!"? We certainly have. We've encountered that vacant stare, that low-energy, borderline catatonic state, that person who wants you to believe they're focused on your every word, that CEO who's just lulled everyone to sleep. We've witnessed the slip of the elbow off the table, the head drop, the answering of a question no one asked. Oh so awkward and spectacular!

Wouldn't it be great to work for a company that invited you to participate? A company that understood your buy-in would be far greater if you were able to contribute to solutions? We're experiencing a new reality in our organizations today—a continuous storm of change that won't end any time soon. This storm has rocked our stability, picked up the pace and created different demands for leaders and members of our organizations. Yet we continue with our old mindsets and antiquated ways. We cling to control, sacrificing relationships for compliance and purpose for power and position. We spend an inordinate amount of time on change efforts that fail over 70% of the time, that don't yield the promised results or that deliver unintended and even harmful consequences. This results in more time spent managing the impact of the unwanted effects of our change initiatives. Organizations are caught in vicious cycles of change without seeing or experiencing the benefits of improvement: better work life, service levels and overall performance. People burn out and become demoralized. Relationships are broken. Fear, turmoil and irrationality ensue.

A new pathway is needed for leaders in today's organizations. This journey begins by recognizing that our world is different now. We live in a complex, network-driven era during a sociotechnical revolution. New models of leadership are required to achieve the service levels and value-based outcomes expected in today's world. The leader's focus must change. A leader must move from decision-maker to catalyst for effective decisions and actions from team members.

This type of leadership needs a new way of thinking. It needs a reframing of our mental models—new points of view that fit our current circumstances. When we're able to reframe our views, we discover the extent to which our preferences are outdated and frame-bound, rather than reality-bound. We take in information and attach new meaning to it. We change our beliefs, ideas and attitudes. This reframing is an experiential process by which we begin to adapt to a changing world willingly and deeply, not knowing where the path will lead. Reframing requires vulnerability and loosening our grip on the security blanket to which we tightly cling. This is a call to recognize the #StupidGoneViral and learn a new way.

This isn't your mother's world

Do you ever feel as if the world's gone mad? The word "mad" often comes to mind as we listen to the news and encounter the dynamics of our times both personally and professionally. The quick evolution of several major technological and sociological forces has resulted in massive change, uncertainty and complexity. Systemization and globalization, along with the knowledge explosion, technological innovation, demographic shifts, regulatory restructuring and environmental pressures, have conspired to continually reshape how we live and work.

*

It's a mad, mad, mad world

*

Systemization and globalization are the connecting of people, enterprises and fortunes across multiple entities—or in the case of globalization, across national boundaries. They create new networks. Our focus expands from the local dynamics only, to include the smooth functioning of the system (or organization) across a borderless market. Loyalties are to the system rather than to the more local, regional or national context (Rothkopf 2008). This refocus and approach often requires the sacrifice of autonomy and creativity for standardization across multiple entities to achieve reliability and economies of scale. And this standardization often comes at a cost to the human spirit when compliance, rather than creativity, becomes the order of the day.

Another significant force of disruption is the knowledge explosion. The amount of information in the world is increasing at unprecedented speeds through connection and digitization. As information grows, so does complexity. As complexity grows, we find ourselves needing more information and knowledge (Bennet & Bennet 2004). This cycle reveals the need to move away from the expert-solutions approach, or the belief that there are experts with the answers to today's problems. Rather, we need a learning approach—an approach based on the premise that there are many right answers and ways to solve a problem. But these ways require intention and learning within the context in which the problem exists.

The technological forces at work are the capacity to connect regardless of physical location, the abundance and availability of data, information and knowledge, and the speed in which transactions and/or services can occur. We can work from just about anywhere and stay connected. In fact, at the time of this writing, we (the authors) are working as senior executives and consultants, commuting physically and connected electronically across the country. We're able to stay connected and present not only from our local offices, but also while driving down the expressway and traveling in the air.

FORCES OF CHANGE

- Systemization
- Globalization
- Knowledge explosion
- Technological innovation
- Demographic shifts
- Regulatory restructuring
- Environmental pressures

✳

*Where, oh where, has my
sanity gone?*

✳

Sociotechnical forces also contribute to the avalanche of change and growing complexity and uncertainty. Family structures are evolving with climbing divorce rates, more single-parent households and scattered families. Many of us have had to re-examine the meaning of family and family identity and create a new paradigm of family that gives us meaning, purpose and direction. This is not our mother's world.

The growth of urban America and societal values of independence and competition have led to greater fragmentation, polarization, individualism and materialism. The longest economic downturn since the Great Depression has led to bankruptcies, foreclosures, defaults and deflation. Government has become more involved in regulating several important industries, such as education, banking, automobiles, insurance and healthcare. The overall population is aging, and we're seeing four generations of workers in the workplace and a tsunami of retirements on the horizon.

And let's not forget that there's a whole new way of communicating out there: emojis, chatspeak, texting acronyms and abbreviations—LOL, OMG, MYOB, etc. Gone are the days of writing a few grammatically correct sentences or, even more antiquated, writing something with a pen on paper. Now, we eliminate punctuation and text our friends using emojis and slang. With a little help from Webopedia, we can all look cool. ICYMI 4YO WTWPC2. (In case you missed it, and for your information, we think we're pretty cool, too!)

Getting back to the science. Each of these trends has exponentially increased the amount of change and uncertainty we experience daily. And the changes keep coming faster. We no longer have the luxury of rest or the feeling of a job well done before the next wave approaches. We find ourselves emotionally shifting back and forth between wanting a sense of belonging and moving toward isolation to preserve our individual freedom and sanity. Each generation handles this emotional shifting differently, adding new layers of intergenerational complexity and conflict.

Growing complexity in the workplace

Organizations are complex systems. They have many diverse and changing parts (e.g., people, roles, professions, regulations, laws, products, infrastructure, etc.) that interact and impact each other in multiple ways. But together, they focus on a common purpose. For example, a city is a system. At the most basic level, the common purpose of a city's population is to live safely. In an organization, the common purpose is the "why" behind the organization's existence—its mission. The greater the diversity of its members and the greater the impact one's actions has on others, the greater the complexity of the system.

Complexity introduces new risks into a system, some seen and some hidden, some organizational and some personal. These new risks often result in unintended behaviors to protect personal interests and the status quo. But a system cannot thrive when its members act in their own interest rather than the interest of the whole. Imagine your right foot refusing to respond to your brain's message to apply pressure to the brake as you approach a cliff. Or imagine a nation of people with a split identity—one group wants independence and the other wants to stay with the status quo (e.g., the Brexit scenario). Or, increasingly common, imagine some individuals or groups having a particular racial, religious, ethnic, social, professional or cultural identity and acting out of that identity to promote their own interests or concerns without regard for the interests or concerns of the larger group.

At a time when we need to embrace our diversity to work through the rapid changes coming at us, we're becoming increasingly distracted and thrown off course by the "identity mindset" in the workplace. The emotion this mindset projects is outrage. It doesn't seek to first understand the nuances or even the truth of specific situations. It becomes a lazy habit of rushing to judgment without the facts. It tarnishes intentions and reputations—generalizes, categorizes, condemns and shuts the dialogue down.

*

I'm outraged that you're outraged . . . Really?

*

As organizations acquire a diverse workforce linked across distances, generations, cultures and subcultures, it becomes more critical and more difficult to have a cohesive purpose and an understanding of the whole. As the number of interactions and transactions increase, so does the complexity, and so does the need for each interaction to be focused on the right things to achieve the purpose. We realize this is easier said than done. Sometimes it's difficult to even know who our employees are (they're on-site, off-site, contracted, full-time, part-time and per diem) let alone understand their contributions to and impact on the organization. A minor change in one department can significantly affect other parts of the organization or the whole without the change agent realizing or intending it.

Managing complexity is at the heart of leadership in our organizations today. It requires a contemporary understanding of people and systems—the dynamics of humans and their relationships and the dynamics of complex adaptive systems. This is where our journey begins.

 ## Keeping it real

COMPLEXITY: LET'S PUT SOME LIPSTICK ON IT

My trek into complexity began with a small town of about 9,000 in the Midwest—a town where everyone knows your name and doors are never locked. Growing up, I had a great life that was pretty uncomplicated.

Then it was off to college. Upon graduation, I felt pulled to the big city of Washington, DC. I packed up my car (a manual transmission I'd yet to master) and headed out for the adventure with eyes and mind wide open. I was full of fear of the unknown but excited to experience all that a vibrant, busy city has to offer.

Little did I know how little I knew. One of the first challenges was learning to drive in the city during rush-hour traffic. In my small town, there might have been a rush moment—but nothing like a rush hour that went on for hours (plural)! Multiple people screamed and honked at me. I thought they were just excited to see me until a person zipped up next to my car with hand signals that were anything but friendly. This city stuff was already providing a new education.

Then there was my first day of work riding the Metro (we didn't have a subway system in my hometown). There was so much to know and the maps were so confusing with their multiple colors for multiple lines. When the train appeared, I acted as if I knew what I was doing and hopped on board. As the train moved along, the conductor announced that we were on our way to Boston—at least that's what I heard. I immediately panicked and get off at the next station trying to figure out where I'd gone wrong. We were really on our way to Ballston. The accents were so different—and my ears had yet to adapt. I got back on the train in the hopes that I was headed in the right direction and realized, all too late, that I had followed the crowd to the wrong side of the track and was now headed in the wrong direction. By the time this was all worked out, I was two hours late for my first day at work. Undoubtedly a fantastic first impression!

Then it was time for lunch from a food truck—so many smells to choose from (some good, some bad)—which I ate on a perfect bench in Lafayette Park, directly across from the White House. Thinking I was so cool in my fabulous work clothes and matching pink high heels, I proceeded to stare in wonderment at the historical site with a feeling of amazement about my new life. Suddenly, I felt a wet sensation on my feet! I looked to my left and saw that someone was yelling at me, telling me he hated my shoes, and relieving himself all over them. I'm sure you can imagine what I was thinking: WTF! Who could do something like this? If you've been to DC, you'll know that things like this can be commonplace. But this sure wasn't commonplace for me! Once the shock and disgust wore off, I found a fountain and attempted to discreetly rid myself of the nasty!

I returned to my office by a peculiar route as I got lost in all the twists and turns of the high-rise jungle. Geez . . . Life in the city was much more difficult than it was in my hometown. The communication styles and expectations were different. The pace was different. Nothing looked familiar. I felt a bit unhinged without any of my usual supports in place.

My story is similar to that of many organizations today. They start out as that small-town girl—smart, full of promise and sure of the way. And over time, they find themselves in a world that's much more complex than anticipated. In DC, I learned quickly that if I continued with my old ways, I wouldn't survive. I needed to adapt and learn the ways of this new and complex world to make it through the day. I willingly threw myself into it, figured things out through trial and error and eagerly made the changes I needed to not just survive, but thrive.

⋆ Titter time: Stupid gone viral ⋆

"If I died and went to hell, it would take me a week to realize I wasn't at work anymore."
—Unknown

Self-Help

A key complexity principle is that the future is truly unknowable, so we must learn to live and deal with uncertainty, surprise, paradoxes and complexity.

Take a few minutes to reflect on these questions:

- Are there any uncertainties keeping you awake at night? If so, what are they?

  _____

  _____

  _____

  _____

- Have you experienced any surprises this past year that threw you off course and/or that you're having a difficult time recovering from? Describe the experience(s).

  _____

  _____

  _____

  _____

- Do you have any competing priorities in your life that you feel are creating a no-win situation? For instance, if you respond to one priority, you negatively impact the other? Describe this dilemma.

_____

_____

_____

_____

_____

_____

_____

_____

As our world becomes increasingly complex, we'll experience more and more uncertainty. The good news—this is normal. The even better news—managing uncertainty personally and professionally requires new ways of living and leading that can be learned. Stay tuned as we continue this journey together.

2
Are You Talking To Me?
A Call For Transformation:
The L3 Fusion Model

Ever have a moment where a colleague takes you to the edge of the patience cliff? In sheer exasperation, you say that phrase you hated to hear most as a child—"The level of your obnoxious is obnoxious." You're aghast to discover that you delivered it exactly as your mother did. You're a failure! You look around the office to see if she's come back to haunt you. Unfortunately, the answer is no. You willingly followed her right down that path. You realize *now* is the moment to make a change and remove that from your management toolkit. We've all been there. It's time for a new way of thinking, and you're on a mission!

The L3 Fusion Model: A journey to transformation

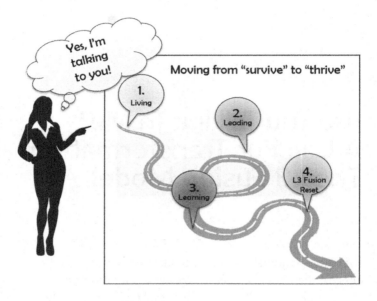

It's increasingly understood within many US industries and the public domain that our systems need to transform to survive. This transformation, or radical change, requires two major efforts: (1) a fundamental change in the underlying beliefs and assumptions that perpetuate the current system, and (2) a fundamental redesign of many of the component parts (Scott & Steinbinder 2009). Each of these major efforts requires a shift in our thinking and actions that includes how we lead, manage ourselves and manage our relationships. It also requires a shift in how we view ourselves, others and our organizations. What got us here won't get us there.

Shift change

The L3 Fusion Model is an emerging theory of leadership that's grounded in the sciences—the sciences of complex adaptive systems, high reliability, psychology and implementation. In this model, leadership is purpose-centric, rather than power- or position-centric. This purpose is fundamental and creates an identity that influences our thoughts, choices and interactions as well as the design of the system itself.

This is a transformational model. It requires more than surface-level change. It goes much deeper into exploring our inner, personal beliefs and values. When a fundamental change occurs in our inner world, our identity as a leader is transformed, bringing about a change in our character through the integration of new understandings. Austrian-American physicist and systems scientist Fritjof Capra (1982) writes of this transformation experience with an analogy of the sweetness of sugar. He reminds us that sugar is made up of three types of atoms—oxygen, hydrogen and carbon. The sweetness of sugar, however, is not a product of any one atom individually, nor is it simply a product of the molecule. It is a sensory experience that emerges from the interaction and integration of the molecule and our taste buds. The sweetness, therefore, is in the relationship.

✶

The sweetness is in the relationship

✶

Similarly, through the integration of the L3 Fusion Model's principles and concepts, a new paradigm of transformational leadership will emerge. The model is made up of three components—healthy living, leading and learning. When these diverse components are fused into a single model of leadership, energy is released into the organization and the sweetness of new thoughts, actions, interactions and structures emerge.

Grit and grace

Leadership in this evolving paradigm is an inside-out experience of both grit and grace. It's leadership that acknowledges the importance of honoring ourselves and others while influencing the system to get the desired results.

To have grit is to act with firmness of mind and spirit in the face of difficulty. Grit is about staying focused on the purpose while navigating the opportunities and obstacles along the way. Grit is principled, tenacious and tough-minded. Grit gets it done.

To have grace is to act with kindness, generosity and suspended judgment. It's restorative and transformational, touching the human spirit. Grace leads with the understanding that everyone is important and has something unique to contribute, regardless of their position, gender, ethnicity or socioeconomic status. Grace unearths the talent and gets it to the table.

While grit and grace are fundamental to this journey, they aren't enough. The organizations we work in today are complex, difficult to understand, rapidly changing, full of diversity and have cultures that are often harmful. They are complex systems—not the stable, mechanistic, predictable organizations of the past. While leading with grit and grace we must also become systems thinkers to anticipate and navigate the world of complexity.

Seeking clarity in a not-so-obvious world

The L3 Fusion Model is built on systems and system thinking. It's important to understand the fundamentals of organizational systems and how they work as we begin this journey.

An organizational system is a group of elements—people, functions, relationships, attributes, technology, other pieces and parts—that together have a specific purpose, such as to deliver a service or product. This purpose allows one to distinguish whether an element (which can be anything) is inside or outside the system.

Systems evolve over time. They are dynamic. To survive, they must adapt faster than the external environment demands.

Systems have boundaries that separate them from other systems. Boundaries may be open to interactions in the environment (such as a loose network of volunteers) or closed (such as a special-ops military system). If boundaries are too open, the organization can lose its identity and sense of purpose. If too closed, it loses flexibility.

Organizational systems have inputs from the outside (people, energy, talent, materials) that must be transformed into outputs that add value (such as products and services). The quality and quantity of these inputs can significantly affect the quality and quantity of the outputs (results).

Organizational systems have all sorts of information and feedback loops that influence and impact decision-making and how the work gets done. The feedback can result in anything from reinforcing the status quo to creating new ideas, products and energy for innovation.

Organizational systems also have decision-making structures that help them maintain stability and survive. These structures can be anywhere from detrimental to highly effective, from too rigid and top-down to too flexible and uncoordinated or chaotic.

Complex organizational systems have many interdependent and moving parts. When one part/person/function changes, the rest of the systems are influenced in ways that aren't well understood. The boundaries are more open, so there's a large and constant exchange of information. No one person can know or comprehend the actions and effects operating within the whole system. As a result, many mistaken assumptions inform the work.

To navigate our complex organizations effectively, we need a fundamental change in our thinking and a redesign of the way we lead.

The L3 Fusion journey begins

Regardless of where you are on your life, leadership and learning journey, it's time to reconsider what's healthy, important, restorative and effective. In other words, now is the time to summon the courage to move beyond surviving to thriving.

The L3 Fusion Model is an antidote for impotent living and leading. It's a journey, not a destination. A marathon, not a sprint. It's messy because it involves learning. Many of us have expertise that's no longer relevant. Giving it up is hard. Becoming a novice again makes us feel vulnerable. Welcome to the world of transformation!

The model starts with "me"—who I am, how I think, the choices I make, the behaviors I exhibit and how I nurture my relationships: #It'sAllAboutMe.

A healthier me creates a healthier work environment and allows for healthier leadership. But it's not enough.

The L3 Fusion Model also introduces transformational principles and skills that are critical for creating healthy organizations—organizations that can successfully change and adapt. The model integrates systems thinking into the transformational leadership model through seven lenses: organizational vision, culture and behaviors, leadership, teams, structures, performance measurement and learning.

We go well beyond scientific evidence and theory. We also share our experiences from the field through stories that illustrate the good, the bad and the ugly. We arm you with new tools, skills and techniques to help you integrate your learning into real-world leading.

Lastly, we present you with a call to action for ongoing learning and transformation through a broader network of support for yourself and with others. When we're willing to learn and practice these new ways together, we become better able to create "islands of sanity" (Wheatley 2017, p. 49)—places where people are more willing to respond and engage because they feel honored and supported rather than dehumanized.

 ## Keeping it real

THE PURPLE-VAN TRANSFORMATION

Do you ever find yourself thinking about that aha moment that changed everything for you? We've all had them. They come in unique flavors, shapes and sizes. Some come through quick and deeply personal moments of insight. Some come slowly, through multiple experiences and reflections on those experiences. And others occur through a highly charged emotional experience or crisis. But all aha moments result in a change in both our beliefs and actions.

As a young girl, I was anxious to have my first date. I was operating under a "no dating before you turned sixteen" rule, so as soon as I celebrated my sweet sixteen, I was determined to go on a date—no matter my options. As luck would have it, a friend wanted to go out with a guy she was crushing on and he was willing to go if she found a date for his friend. Hmmmm . . . I should have known this was too good to be true, but being stubborn and anxious, I agreed. Of course, being so excited, I failed to get any details. Later, I would realize this was a *very* important misstep.

When the Saturday night arrived, my date pulled up (without my friend) in a large purple van. Not what I'd expected, but I was still optimistic. He greeted my father with a "Hey, man"—and in true fatherly fashion, my dad asked that he call him "sir" and stated the rules: back by 11:00 p.m., "no funny business," etc. I wasn't happy that my friend was nowhere to be found, but I remained hopeful and proceeded to whip past my parents with a speedy goodbye (I was sooo cool).

Once we were on the road, my date didn't have much to say. Our destination was Bloomington, which was where everyone went to have fun on the weekends. I just knew I was on my way to being uber cool. But the van remained excruciatingly quiet, no matter what interesting fact I tried to impart. At first, I thought he was shy. It soon became apparent he was just a doorknob of a date. When the van slowed down, I looked around and saw that we were at a bait and tackle shop. Certainly not what I'd envisioned. While my date was busy making his purchase, I glanced behind me and noticed that the inside of the van was covered wall-to-wall with bright blue shag carpet, black lights and a host of other things I didn't let myself think about. I wasn't sure what was on the agenda, but my mind did some profound wandering.

Next stop on our adventure was the Wendy's drive-thru. Wait a minute—we drove all the way to Bloomington to pick up bait and now this? Things couldn't get any worse. Wrong! He proceeded to accidentally dump his Frosty and mine all over himself and make a disgusting joke. He then scooped the remaining Frosty back into a cup and insisted I eat it because he didn't want it wasted and it was my dinner. Are you kidding? That was enough for me—time to end this date! I made up an excuse, he turned the van around and we were back where it all began by 7:45 p.m. It was probably the shortest first date in history, but it felt like the longest.

Being ever so polite, I thanked my date for the drive and ran as fast as I could to the door. Dear Dad, standing there with a grin on his face and a twinkle in his eye, asked me if I'd had as much fun as I'd thought I would. Well, no.

It was right then that I had one of my most memorable aha moments. I decided that I would never again be so eager to rush into *anything*. I would take my time and think things through. That thinking has stuck with me. Today, as I evaluate new or unfamiliar situations, I take time to think about the road ahead, about the possible turns and my ability to maneuver them before I make any decision. Reckless eagerness is now placed alongside inquisitive thoughtfulness and the confidence to say no to the purple vans that come along.

✱ *Titter time: It's all about me* ✱

"I'll have a café mocha vodka latte to go, please."
—Unknown

 ## Self-Help

This is a thinking exercise—past, present, future. When we change the way we think about organizations and people, the organizations and people change. Sit back for a few minutes and explore your beliefs (past and present) about the statements below, as well as the implications of these beliefs:

- People in organizations have the freedom to choose

- People support what they create

- The consequences of decisions made in organizations often aren't understood

- Organizations are living systems with the ability to change, adapt and grow

- Organizations have energy that flows and blocks and moves around obstacles and creates patterns

- Organizational diversity is critical to effectively respond to external demands

We'll explore these concepts in more depth as we reframe our thinking about the future.

_____

_____

_____

_____

_____

_____

_____

_____

_____

_____

_____

_____

_____

_____

3

The Struggle Is Real: Leading Well Starts With Living Well

You likely know the feeling of being out of control. How many times have you forgotten (or almost forgotten) to pick up your child at school? Or, while driving and stressing out over work deadlines, homework, soccer practice, etc., forgotten that your child is in the back seat when a troll just happens to hit your car from behind. You react like a mother tiger and, in your shock, let loose a few unkind words—only to have the teacher call you later that day from the school. She's wondering why your four-year-old said that he was late for school because "A f*er hit Mommy's car."

This was your living-on-the-edge moment. It's time to take back control and redefine your purpose!

The L3 Fusion Model:
A journey to transformation

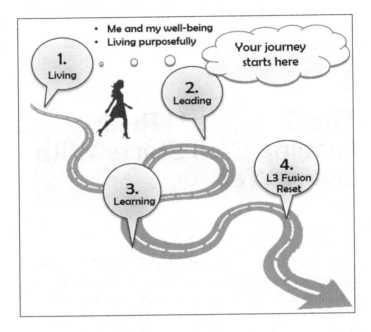

Our behavior, and therefore our relationships and performance, is shaped by many interconnected and dynamic factors in our personal and professional lives. These behavioral influences include:

- The choices we make in the past and present

- The knowledge, skills and abilities we possess

- Personal factors, such as health, energy and personal conflicts

- Our perceptions of risk and competing priorities

- The cultures in which we live and work

- The system factors within our lives, such as support structures, incentives, rules, regulations and controls (Griffith 2019)

We're often unaware of how these behavioral influences impact our personal and professional lives. And when we're not clear about who we are and where we're going, these factors can throw us off course and toss us to and fro as if we were a rudderless boat in the wind. It's important, therefore, to have a sense of who we are when we're at our best self, when we're whole, working within our strengths, experiencing our true north.

Too often we encounter leaders who make us shake our heads (almost uncontrollably) because it's hard to fathom how unaware of themselves they are. For instance, you have a "leader" who believes they *must* be involved in everything; they're the glue when it comes to project management. Nope—not happening. This particular leader is actually the worst at project management. They're extraordinarily nervous, they stress over every word, every sentence, every conversation, every meeting—the list goes on. They're exhausted and exhausting, and the project hasn't even begun! They may have some great skills, but refusing to recognize their own weakness(es) is what makes them a lackluster leader and results in a frustrated and demotivated team.

This lackluster leader's performance is shaped by many factors that she doesn't see or understand. She believes she has great project-management skills. Being risk averse, she believes that if the team doesn't meet her expectations, there will be hell to pay, including financial penalties. She thinks that relationships are secondary to getting the job done, and getting the job done is central to her self-esteem. And sadly, her team intuitively knows this and responds by shutting down their creative juices and doing what they need to do to simply survive. Sucks to be you!

There's a strong link between an organization's success and the emotional intelligence of its leaders. And the more complex the job, the more emotional intelligence matters. Peter Senge (1990), director of the Organizational Learning Center at Massachusetts Institute of Technology, concluded that people with high levels of personal mastery "cannot afford to choose between reason and intuition or the head and heart, any more than they would choose to walk on one leg or see with one eye" (p. 168). When it comes to everyday decision-making, intuition (or gut feelings) provides critical information for effective performance. This awareness of our feelings and tendencies is the fundamental emotional competence. It's the ability to focus on internal meters and subtle signals and effectively use them, along with the objective facts, to guide our performance.

Finding your purpose: Compass, GPS or map?

Living purposefully is about choosing to do things based on an inner sense of rightness, wholeness, truth. It's intentional living. It's about being grounded, being centered or having a true north. Without a sense of purpose, we can't tell where we are or why we're here. The only certainty is overwhelming ambiguity. We lose our sense of the definite. And in time, we lose our sense of true self (Herman 1997). It's too easy to lose our sense of self when we're in personal-crisis mode (death, divorce, terminal illness, etc.). We think we're managing, and by theoretically staying engaged, we believe we're distracting ourselves from the crisis when, in fact, we're just piling on. We're running on high emotional drain and have extreme reactions to the most basic of problems, which ultimately leads to thinking everyone is out to get us. "The problem can't be with me—it's with everyone else." The struggle is real! Purposeful living becomes an imperative to a healthier you: #LivePurposefully.

Think about living purposefully as having a compass. The compass doesn't specifically tell us where to go, as a GPS system would (e.g., turn right, go 200 feet, and then turn left). And it doesn't help us understand the context/terrain of the available paths, as a map would. Rather, a compass points us in the right direction. There may be multiple paths and stop-off points along the way, but the compass always points to true north.

Our truth is the fusion of our values, beliefs, passions and strengths within this inner core. Our truth brings us energy, vitality and meaning. Our truth keeps us steady in times of uncertainty. There may be times that our path is clear, or even times when we feel an inner or divine guidance. But most often our truth is about becoming aware of what's important to us. We are living purposefully when we routinely check in with ourselves and make choices that align with this truth.

There is no one alive who is youer than you.
—Dr. Seuss

Boundaries and choices

Boundary setting is an important aspect of focusing on what's important to us. A boundary is anything that helps differentiate us from someone else or shows where we begin and end. We deal with physical boundaries every day. Our skin is a physical boundary, as are fences, guideposts, ditches and walls. They respectively protect our body, define our property, mark our path, keep us out of dangerous areas and create spaces for various activities.

We also have intangible boundaries. Choosing well and staying aligned with our inner truth requires the daily practice of setting intangible boundaries, or guardrails. These guardrails keep us on track, define us and honor this truth. We live more purposefully when we set boundaries that help us:

- Keep things that will nurture us inside our internal fence

- Keep things that will harm us outside this fence

Examples of intangible boundaries include our words, especially the word *no*, and the emotional distance we create with those who bring us down. Other intangible boundaries include the rules we create for ourselves to keep us on the right path—rules about social media usage, exercise, diet, sex, response times for e-mails or texts when angry, etc. Let's bring it back to everyday struggles.

SPEAKING OF BOUNDARIES—THE POO PACT

Do you ever find yourself dreaming of enjoying peace and quiet in the privacy of your own bathroom? You just want those few minutes in the day to reflect on the "whatever." Invariably, right as you're beginning to have your moment, the door opens and your kids barge in wanting you to help with a math problem or break up an argument. And if you're lucky, they've brought along a friend and the dog. They're completely oblivious to the fact that Mom might be busy with something else! Or your significant other has a burning question that requires an immediate response. Really? It couldn't wait until you'd enjoyed those precious five minutes?

Thankfully, there's a solution. You may have heard through social media about a new trend in bathroom privacy etiquette called the "poo pact." You decide it's time for your own pact—all it needs is to be designed and implemented. The guardrails are defined, and interruptions and negotiations become a thing of the past! What could be more brilliant?

We've talked to so many leaders across the country who have no true sense of who they are or where they're going. They work for a paycheck, or for status, or to minimize their risks. They're rudderless, going from one fad, one job, one position to the next. They're adrift, joyless, despondent.

> All my life I wanted to be somebody. Now I realize I should have been more specific.
> —Jane Wagner

In *Find Your Strongest Life*, author Marcus Buckingham (2009) identifies two significant trends from survey data collected from more than 1.3 million men and women over the last thirty years in the US and developed countries around the world: over the last few decades, women have become less happy with their lives; and as women get older, they get sadder. These trend lines are "moving in the opposite direction from what you would predict given women's dramatic advances in education, employment opportunities, earning power and societal/political influence" (p. 26). Buckingham attributes much of this unhappiness to the multiple choices we have in our lives combined with a lack of intentional discrimination when it comes to choosing the right things daily.

The trend for men is unsettling, as well. A recent study on happiness found that men are less happy than women when they're younger and become happier over time when they attain success in personal finance and marriage (Plagnol & Easterlin 2008). In our unstable economic times and in an era of high divorce rates, it's difficult to get too optimistic about the growing happiness of men.

We all find ourselves overwhelmed and distracted by everyday living. While choice is a matter of freedom and power, our indiscriminate and non-intentional everyday choices sap our energy, keep our relationships at arm's length and create a sense of overwhelming anxiety and despondency.

When we live out of our purpose, however, we're able to bring our unique personality, passions, thoughts and actions into everyday living and leading; we work out of our strengths. We focus less on fixing our deficits and more on the many possibilities. When we're focused on the possibilities, we receive more power to move into these possibilities. This gives us a sense of freedom and hope for both the short term and the long.

My health impacts my performance

We can't talk about healthy lifestyles without talking about habits that impact us physically, emotionally and spiritually. To achieve a healthy lifestyle, it's important to focus on these five areas:

- Purposeful living—choosing to do things based on your inner sense of rightness, wholeness, truth

- Exercise—having a daily routine of physical activity that helps improve physical and mental fitness

- Nutrition—eating food that's needed for healthy growth and repair

- Interpersonal support—having a person and / or network of people to interact with and who provide practical and / or emotional support

- Stress management—having and using tools and techniques to control your stress levels and improve everyday functioning

Before looking ahead, it's helpful to look back at our old patterns, triggers, distortions, obstacles and setbacks. Turn around. What do you see? Are there any red flags or recurring themes to give you some insights into your personal health?

We often meet people struggling with their emotional health on their leadership journey. Some don't recognize their symptoms while others simply choose to ignore them, minimizing their importance or value. For example, we met a young woman who confessed to becoming sick every morning as she drove up the hill toward her office complex. Routinely, she'd throw up a couple of times before going inside and would shake until she got to her office and closed the door. She told us she'd pray that no one would come in to ask her a question. This woman's unhealthy reaction to her work environment impacted her physical and mental health, as well as her relationships with her peers and supervisor (e.g., she was despondent in meetings, only interacted via e-mail, avoided team-building activities, etc.). Rather than look inward to determine the problem and address it, she often blamed others for her anxiety.

The easiest part of leadership is having the right technical skills and knowledge to get the work done. The most difficult part is knowing and managing ourselves and our relationships in ways that help people move forward. This requires some emotional intelligence. Have you often thought about how much easier your job would be if you didn't have to deal with people? Yes, we hear it often.

Emotional intelligence isn't a new concept. Psychologists have studied the abilities and skills associated with emotional intelligence for many years, and there's an impressive and growing body of research suggesting that these abilities are important for success in work performance and life in general.

Emotional intelligence refers to the capacity for recognizing our own feelings and the feelings of others, for motivating ourselves and for managing emotions effectively within ourselves and our relationships. Emotional competence encompasses the skills and abilities to do the same. Managing relationships requires five basic emotional and social competencies (Goleman 1998):

- Self-awareness: knowing what we're feeling in the moment and understanding these feelings well enough to help guide decision-making; being able to realistically assess our own abilities; having a well-grounded sense of self-confidence

- Self-regulation: handling our emotions in a way that allows us to facilitate rather than interfere with the task at hand; being conscientious and delaying gratification to pursue goals; recovering well from emotional distress

- Motivation: using our deepest preferences to move and guide us toward our goals, to help us take initiative and strive to improve, and to persevere in the face of setbacks and frustrations

- Empathy: sensing what people are feeling; being able to understand others' perspectives; cultivating rapport with a broad range of people

- Social skills: handling emotions well in relationships and reading social situations and networks accurately; interacting smoothly; using these skills to persuade and lead, negotiate and settle disputes

Emotional competence is a set of skills that can be learned. This learning process begins with exploring our dreams, values, assumptions and expectations—some of which are faulty. Self-exploration helps us become more aware of what makes us think and act the way we do. Self-awareness is the starting point of the emotional competence journey and facilitates empathy and self-management, which are both critical for effective leadership.

The simple truth is that our health (physical, emotional, spiritual) is our responsibility. And when we invest in our wellness, the world becomes a healthier place for us to exist in. A personal coach or therapist can help us learn the skills needed to identify and manage our emotions, meditation can help us be calm and centered and regular exercise just makes us feel good all the way around. All these things allow us and everyone around us to benefit from less stress and more engagement.

When we pay attention to our health, we shift our priorities. We become more purposeful. As we practice this shift, we change our habits. This shift often leads to the ability to better negotiate, manage, and adapt to the world around us. We're better able to recover from setbacks, stay engaged in our lives and experience joy. Be open to taking that first step toward change—we guarantee you're worth the investment!

Keeping it real

PERFECTION ISN'T THE GOAL

Some of us have struggled with perfectionism our whole lives. Maybe your parents expected (quite frankly demanded) perfection. And when you didn't deliver, there were consequences. So what did you do? Became stressed, obsessed and sometimes even ill trying to achieve perfection. This carried over into your work life, where you now try to please everyone or achieve perfection first time out of the chute—impossible! First of all, it's a moving target. What pleases someone one day will change in fifteen minutes, an hour, the next day, etc. Secondly, it is often more important to execute a 'good enough' solution that gets the process going rather than delay the launch because it isn't perfect. Perfection isn't the goal. Living authentically, striving to be true to our inner purpose and getting results is.

KNOW WHEN TO APOLOGIZE

When we fail to be perfect, many of us immediately apologize. "Sorry I didn't live up to your expectations"; "Sorry I didn't pass that exam"; "Sorry I wasn't able to solve that problem"; "Sorry I lost that promotion." It's endless. Stop apologizing for imperfection. Take a step back and see what can be learned from the situation.

GOOD IS GOOD ENOUGH

Until we take stock and realize that we can't be everything to everyone, or that we won't be perfect at everything and that most times good is good enough, this vicious cycle will continue. Too often, trying to be everything to everyone results in a life more focused on reaching the goal regardless of personal cost instead of appreciating the journey toward that goal. We can learn from both, but which one is more enlightening, more engaging, more fun, more focused on the whole? Unrelenting focus can result in less engagement at work and a willingness to take the easy path forward. When we avoid failure, we also avoid learning.

WHAT DOESN'T KILL ME MAKES ME STRONGER

Yes, failure comes with consequences (e.g., a project wasn't successful, you lost the promotion, you got fired, etc.). They can be horrible on the surface, especially when we're right in the middle of the situation. But you've heard this before—how we react to our failures is what makes us stronger as leaders and as people in general. Learning and recovering from our failures is key. Maintaining perspective, managing our stress, interacting cooperatively, asking for feedback and supporting and building our networks help build our resilience.

CHANGE YOUR PERSPECTIVE

We must realize that we have the power to define ourselves. Don't let others try to define you—especially not parents and bosses. They can mentor you, they can teach you, but they don't define you. Quite often we get caught up in trying to be the person that we or others think we should be. Simple example—I'm a horrible baker and every year my daughter's grade school asked parents to bake cookies for various events. I bought mine, and one time when I proudly delivered them, the room mother said with disgust, "You can't even bake a plate of cookies? Store-bought is just so unhealthy!" I laughed it off but later began to feel horrible that I didn't bake and wasn't the perfect mom. Then my daughter reminded me that my store-bought cookies were the first to go. Keep it in perspective!

KNOW THYSELF

It's best to have this knowledge sooner rather than later, but don't fear—there's always time to get on that bus and understand the journey of you! Don't be that person who insists they're the smartest in the room. Acknowledging our strengths and weaknesses is the first step in knowing ourselves more fully.

⋆ *Titter time: Self-care* ⋆

"My grandmother started walking five miles a day when she was sixty. She's ninety-seven now, and we don't know where the hell she is."
—Ellen DeGeneres

 Self-Help

Happiness is a choice. The foundation of this happiness is discovering and honoring your inner truth. To discover your inner truth and make intentional choices to guide your daily life, ask yourself:

- What do I value and assign importance to?

  _____

  _____

  _____

- What are my strengths and talents?

  _____

  _____

  _____

- In past relationships, what distorted ideas
  did I have about the person involved? Is
  this a pattern?

  _____

  _____

  _____

  _____

- When I experience joy, what are the
  circumstances?

  _____

  _____

  _____

  _____

- How often do I rescue someone from the
  consequences of their own behavior? How
  does this make me feel?

  _____

  _____

  _____

  _____

- When I say no, am I saying no to things that will take me away from what I think is truly important? Can others manipulate me into saying yes when I think I should say no?

  _____

  _____

  _____

- Do I respect others' boundaries, or do I attempt to force my opinions or desires on them? Do I respect their no?

  _____

  _____

  _____

- This past week, what percentage of my waking time was spent on non-intentional activities that took me away from what I value and assign importance to? Where are my opportunities for improvement?

  _____

  _____

  _____

4

I See You: Leaders Nurture Their Relationships

Emotional intelligence is one of our favorite topics. Borderline ridiculous experiences happen all the time. For instance, an executive walks into a room and greets the executive he'll be pitching for financial backing, saying, "You look fantastic—I didn't know you were pregnant!" Well, she wasn't! And this executive just keeps going. "Well if you were, you would look fantastic!" Does this mean since she isn't pregnant, she doesn't look fantastic? The emotional incompetence keeps rolling along . . .

Or there's the executive who's in a board meeting and sees one of his female colleagues turning beet red. Those of us who are menopausal would know that it's just the menopause fairy making her daily visit, but this executive felt the need to loudly say, "Wow, you're turning red—are you okay?" She replies, "I'm fine, it's just a little warm in the room," and slowly slides down in her chair in the hopes of disappearing. Think this executive couldn't possibly be so clueless? Think again. Some people always rise to the occasion! So is it really important to "see" those around you? You bet it is!

The L3 Fusion Model: A journey to transformation

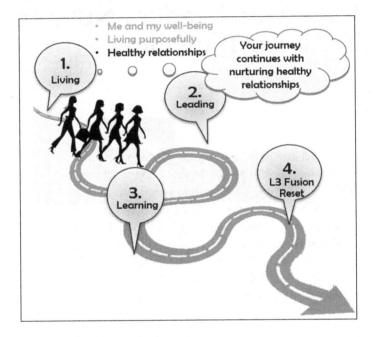

Research has shown that emotional skills are critical for effective relational performance, especially as one moves into higher positions in organizations. Self-awareness is the starting point. If we can't recognize our emotions, we'll be poor at managing them. And if we're oblivious to our own feelings, we'll also tune out how others feel, as in the examples above. By being attuned to how others feel in the moment (social awareness), a leader can say and do what's appropriate, such as calm another's fears or anger, lighten an embarrassing situation and/or join in on the merriment (Goleman, Boyatzis & McKee 2002).

Emotional competence matters twice as much in the workplace as IQ and technical skills because of its positive impact on others and on organizational performance. Studies reveal sharp differences between successful managers and those who derailed (were fired, forced to quit, or reached a plateau) as a result of lack of emotional competence. The two factors most often present when an executive derailed were:

- Rigidity: They were unable to adapt their style to changes in the organizational culture, or unable to take in or respond to feedback about traits they needed to change or improve. They wouldn't listen to or learn from others.

- Poor relationships: The single most frequently mentioned factor was alienating those with whom they worked by being harshly critical, insensitive, or demanding.

This same study (Goleman 1998) showed that technical expertise can be a liability. Most of the managers who failed were technically brilliant. In fact, this technical brilliance was why they were promoted in the first place. But when they reached higher positions in the organization, they had difficulty managing their relationships.

> They won't remember what you said, but they will remember how you made them feel!
> —Carl W. Buehner

Relationships matter

In these times of shifting and uncertain values, we have a special need for supportive, enriching and encouraging relationships in the workplace. A key principle of the L3 Fusion Model is that healthy relationships are critical to our success—no one should go it alone. We all need positive relationships, and they don't just happen. They come about through our investment in others over time—through interactions that convey our values, degree of openness, expertise, experiences and willingness to share and learn. We get a large return when we invest in healthy relationships. They help us become more resilient in times of difficulty. We therefore must steadily build our return on relationships (ROR) to continue moving forward: #BuildYourROR.

While our relationships start with us, they're the responsibility of both parties. I'm responsible for my behavior—managing my emotions, interacting thoughtfully, using my skills of persuasion, cooperation and teamwork, building a positive image—and the other party is responsible for theirs. It's important to remember that a change in our own behavior will impact the behaviors of others. We get the greatest results in our relationships when we focus on our side of the relationship equation—our interactions throughout the day, on stage and off.

In our daily lives, we interact face-to-face and virtually with others multiple times per day (in meetings, hallways, coffee shops, on calls, etc.). We often take these interactions for granted, but they're the foundation of how we do business. Our formal and informal interactions matter. When we consistently present ourselves in a way that represents our genuine thoughts and feelings, we promote stability and trust. When we're inconsistent, we promote the opposite: instability and distrust. Our interactions matter.

Courtesy is an important aspect of strengthening our relationships. It's aided by empathy (the ability to sense others' feelings and/or understand their perspectives) but goes beyond empathy to action. Courtesy is about behaving in a way that shows respect for another person even when we disagree with them or have different beliefs, values, skills, and/or intellectual capabilities. It's not cowardice or shirking away from the reality of a situation. Rather, it's an act of respect toward another human being. Simple courtesies such as a genuine word of encouragement, a thank-you note, an unexpected cup of coffee, a schedule adjustment and other small acts of kindness and affability can smooth the way forward so that relationships are strengthened and information is shared more easily.

We worked with a manager who was struggling with some personal issues. This manager asked her supervisor for a flexible work schedule sporadically, depending on what was going on at home. She was open and honest about her needs as well as her concerns about how a flexible schedule would impact her team members. In the end, her supervisor decided to let her manage her own time, giving her maximum flexibility, with the caveat that the team members and goals wouldn't suffer. The manager got through this difficult time without any negative impact to the team and their goals.

After many years without contact, the two women reconnected. The manager told her former supervisor that she would never forget the kindness shown to her at a time when she needed it most. She described it as "lifesaving." This was a profoundly rewarding moment for the supervisor, who had no idea how important her accommodation had been to this individual and her family. She realized that as leaders we have the power to make or break a situation, and that common courtesy and creativity can go a long way in the human experience.

It's vital to take the time to focus on our relationships, to purposefully nurture them in ways that are thoughtful and genuine, not manipulative or self-centered. Relationship management begins with our authenticity. We must appeal to another as our true self, out of our own purpose and values, while connecting with theirs.

The art of negotiation

All types of relationships require negotiation at times. Negotiation is about coming to a mutual agreement so that things can move forward. It's not haggling or driving the hard bargain and going for as much as you can get. Nor is it being nice or caving in. Negotiation is finding and building common ground as we cooperatively and courteously search for a solution that achieves the goal.

A well-known approach to win-win negotiations was developed by Roger Fisher and William Ury, cofounders of Harvard's Program on Negotiation, and published in the classic book *Getting to Yes* (2011). The evidence-based practices in this book have stood the test of time through an approach called "principled bargaining." Principled bargaining is about achieving an option that's better for everyone, rather than bargaining for a specific position. "Positional bargaining" too often becomes a contest of will with each negotiator asserting what she will or won't do. This type of bargaining strains and destroys relationships.

A key principle of Fisher and Ury's negotiation approach is creating value for both parties—a win-win scenario. They identify four strategies for negotiation that maintain and strengthen relationships through a process of value creation for each party. Their win-win approach is as follows:

- Focus on the problem, not the people. Humans can be unpredictable with easily threatened egos, cognitive biases and blind spots. It's important to understand the other person's thinking and perceptions while exploring the problem at hand. Avoid blaming the problem on them, no matter how tempting. Basically, treat others respectfully as you focus on the problem itself.

- Focus on desires and concerns (interests) not positions. Our desires and concerns motivate us and influence the position we choose. Be firm about your own interests while exploring theirs. Listen, ask questions, be open to their thoughts and suggestions while also attending to your own interests.

- Create multiple options for mutual gain instead of locking in one alternative early on. Brainstorm together and look for new opportunities to achieve the goal. There's more than one way to paint the canvas. Get creative.

- Insist that the result be based on some objective criteria, or standard, versus opinions and subjective concepts. Such standards include safety and quality standards, evidence-based practices, professional standards, procedural standards, etc. Call this out in the beginning and then stick with it.

Negotiation skills are significantly tied to our relationships and leadership outcomes, so everyone benefits when we improve these skills. As we become more self-aware, we're better able to manage our own emotions and the emotions of others. We can get ourselves out of the way so that we can better integrate the evidence-based skills of negotiation.

Develop your posse

Because our world is rapidly changing and complex, it's important to have a trusted network of thought leaders. Building a network takes time, and our network must change over time as our interests and work experiences evolve. It's too easy to avoid doing so, as it takes energy away from other activities. But building a network is critical to our growth. It enriches us.

We encourage thoughtful and purposeful development of this network, not a random approach. It's important to be aware of who's in your network, who should be in it but isn't, and who shouldn't be in it at all.

To build a strong network, you need individuals with expertise and knowledge in your areas of interest, who are accessible and willing to share, who follow through on commitments and who are trustworthy. Make a list of people you would like in your network. Assess the strengths and weaknesses of this group and consider whether the right people are on your network bus. If an individual is closed, dominating, controlling or unethical, take them off the list. If you have strong positive feelings about them, reflect on why and consider adding them to the list. Get the right people on your bus!

Keeping it real

AVOID BIG BUTS

Think back to when someone said they were sorry and it was followed with a nice big "but." We all know people who can't sincerely apologize because it just might be an admission that they did something wrong or hurt someone's feelings—the people who grossly offend and then are unable to self-correct so that both parties are left with some dignity.

For example, say you're a young working mom with two kids. Managing everyday life as well as work has been challenging. You're in a meeting with an executive and he says that the best way women can be helpful is to help their husbands pick out their clothes in the morning. He turns to you and asks you if you help your husband. You don't do this, and he lectures you on how you should be a better partner. Your first reaction is utter dismay, and you think you should stay silent. But this executive just won't let it go. At this point, everyone in the room is listening to this conversation. He continues by telling you many other ways to be a good partner until you blurt out "I'm divorced." Bah-bam. You could hear a pin drop. And then he steps right in that pile of s*&t again and says, "I'm sorry *but* if you want to get married again, you'd better take some notes."

It didn't end there, but you get the gist of where we're going. There's just so much wrong with this big-but scenario. He could have immediately voiced regret, yet he couldn't let himself go there. How sad it is when we're incapable of admitting a wrong and trying to undo the damage. Avoid big buts and don't do "sorry—not sorry."

DON'T GET SUCKED INTO THE UGLY

Consider the times you've worked in an environment that was simply caustic—an environment where gossip and backstabbing were the norm. When we engage in this kind of negativity, we're impacted negatively—regarding how we feel and how we're perceived. This unhealthy behavior is something we should all step away from. (Step away from the car with your hands up!) It's tempting to engage so that we're deemed "part of the in crowd," but doing so only drags us into the dirt, into the ugly.

We each have a choice—to be a positive force or a negative one. And when we rise above this childish and destructive behavior, we feel good, and maybe even a little bit proud of ourselves. Rising above the ugly doesn't mean ignoring it, of course. Sometimes we need to call it out. And sometimes we just need to quietly put our stake in the ground.

✳ Titter time: Relationships ✳

"I'm sorry. I know I said hi, but I wasn't really prepared for any follow-up conversation."
  —Unknown

Self-Help

When building your relationship network, ask yourself:

- Do I belong to a team or community that's accessible to me when I have a problem to solve?

_____

_____

_____

_____

_____

- Do I regularly share my ideas, learnings, and successes with others in my organization, profession or communities of interest?

_____

_____

_____

_____

_____

- Am I available to others who seek my input, and do I avoid the temptation of gossip and backbiting?

  _____

  _____

  _____

  _____

  _____

- What are some practical ways I can nurture my network?

  _____

  _____

  _____

  _____

  _____

5

Hope Is Not A Strategy: Leaders Create The Conditions For Others To Be Successful

Picture this: "Hope Is Not a Strategy" tattooed on every leader's forehead! Wouldn't that solve so many pointless meetings filled with hours of pontificating, positioning and puffery? When in doubt about what to do, these leaders would need only to look in the mirror!

The L3 Fusion Model: A journey to transformation

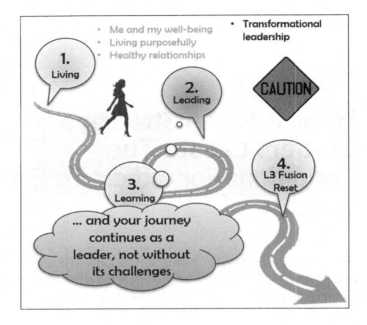

Have you ever felt as if you had a front-row seat to a bad movie while watching lackluster leaders at work? Or have you ever felt as if being a manager put you a heartbeat away from becoming emperor of the universe? Being a leader doesn't mean you have arrived, or that you have special powers or all the answers. Rather, it means you have a unique opportunity to influence others' working conditions. Strong leaders work out of intention, rather than hope, to create the conditions in which others can do their best work and achieve the organization's desired outcomes: #LeadersPrepareTheWay.

True leadership is an attitude, an influence and an activity that makes things happen—things that are in the best interest of a greater purpose.

Leadership isn't a means to an end; it's the means and the end. Leaders at all levels influence people and situations in multiple ways every day—both positively and negatively, knowingly and unknowingly. We can transform a situation simply through the words we use and the language our body speaks. Our smallest intentions and movements can reverberate throughout the organization and even into the community.

Leaders at every organizational level have a huge stake in creating the conditions for success. Employees relate to their immediate supervisor, not the CEO of the company. First-line leaders create many of the conditions that retain and engage their team members on a day-to-day basis. Senior leaders set the overall tone and pace and create the structures that enhance or detract from effective decision-making, problem-solving and actions. Mid-level leaders translate and continuously connect the work and message vertically. And every team member influences the effectiveness of each action throughout the organization. Small actions can make a big difference.

In turbulent times, when organizations are pushed to act faster and perform with more flexibility and efficiency, leadership (formal and informal) is required at all levels of the organization. Hierarchical, top-down approaches aren't adequate. They don't allow for an effective response to the changes required for organizational survival and regeneration. There's simply too much complexity for any one person or executive team to know and understand.

Too often as leaders we fall into the trap of believing we are our role. We dismiss our authentic selves and cling to this illusory leadership identity. We play the toddlers' version of hide-and-seek: if I close my eyes, they can't see me. Or we find ourselves pretending— that we know more, have more skills, have more confidence, have more say. In reality, leaders and their ways are known and incessantly talked about. Our small actions aren't only noticed but also impact the whole, even when we're unaware of them.

In the face of change, uncertainty and growing complexity, we try harder, pretend more. Over time, we become discouraged. We apply old practices to new and complex problems and lose our way. Most of our time is spent fighting fires and managing symptoms while the underlying conditions, or illnesses, continue. Eventually we realize that we're in a vicious cycle. We can either hope (bad strategy), withdraw (not good either) or expose our authentic selves (scary but good) and admit that it's time to learn a new way.

*

Expose yourself to your fears (pants on, please)

*

Several evidence-based principles and associated competencies can help us lead in dynamic organizations. We'll share these with you in more detail in the sections below. But because we know the suspense is killing you, here's a high-level overview. Organizational leaders are most effective when they do these things:

- Set a clear direction, clear limits and a clear pace, mediating between the internal political dynamics and the environmental demands

- Drive responsibility downward to those in the organization who understand the context and have the right expertise

79

- Create environments that promote learning and adaptation

Contemporary leaders demonstrate these principles through their behavior and behavioral expectations of others, through their attention to the organization's culture and vision and by supporting structures, performance-measurement processes and learning strategies.

Leading with clarity

Organizations constantly change. New external demands require new internal responses. Operational stability competes with innovation and growth, creating dynamic tensions, conflicting goals and priorities and competition for resources. And every organization has a political dimension with varying interests and preferences that change the rules of the game as the membership changes. All these dynamics result in conflicting preferences and priorities and changes in the distribution of power and resources. If these dynamics aren't addressed, leaders will find themselves competing rather than collaborating and leading from an outdated playbook at a frenzied pace that seems to be getting them nowhere.

In *Good to Great* (2001), Jim Collins says that the primary indicator of great companies is a focus on not only the strategic goals to be accomplished but also on avoiding and/or ceasing counterproductive activities. Yet our current methods for rolling out new work and change initiatives tend to comprise a "piling on" approach. We don't review the overall business goals and activities, let alone employee and organizational capacity. But each is important in an organization's prioritization and pacing process.

Organizational bandwidth, or capacity, has two components: (1) employee workload and (2) organizational capacity. Employee workload consists of mental and physical demands, time pressure, effort required to reach the desired performance or outcome, degree of perceived frustration and support, and perceived performance. Organizational capacity consists of the hours needed to fully incorporate a new change, as well as the necessary talent, financial resources consumed and expected return on investment (Safar, Defields, Fulop, Dowd & Zavod 2006).

Organizations in the throes of change benefit from regular and formalized attention to employee workload and organizational capacity. This can be achieved through scheduled and structured processes that allow leaders to "pause and look back" at all levels of the organization. Leaders work together to determine the current priorities and timelines for change initiatives. During this process, leaders and participants review the activities, committees and team charters, as well as the intended deliverables, to determine if they're still relevant and on course. We often find that much time is being spent with little return. During this pause, leaders sunset unnecessary or unproductive teams, re-establish priorities and projects and get people back on track. Resources and talent are identified and reassigned to priority projects. And similar activities or initiatives are integrated or bundled in a way that enhances the work and time of the individuals involved (Scott & Mensik 2010).

When we set the direction, our words matter. As leaders, we're constantly communicating important messages to our team members, who come from different career paths, professions, educational levels and walks of life. It's vital to create a common language with our employees to ensure understanding and a level playing field.

Setting a clear direction also involves embracing the many paradoxes we face in organizations, rather than ignoring or denying them. A paradox is a situation in which contradictory features need to be achieved and choosing one makes the other unachievable. For example, organizations strive to achieve both efficiency and innovation. Efficiency requires standardized processes and workflows to minimize variation. Innovation requires time and space for experimenting, creating variation in the system. We cannot focus on one, as the other will fail. As leaders setting a clear direction, we must surface and share these dilemmas, acknowledging the challenges associated with striving for both (a balancing act) and the degree of risk the organization is willing to bear. This provides a framework for ongoing discussions around priorities, competing interests, allocation of resources and expected outcomes.

Driving responsibility downward

The hierarchical leadership that flourished in stable environments isn't effective in today's environments of continuous change and uncertainty. We no longer have the luxury of time. Five-year strategic plans and twelve-month budgets are a thing of the past. Nor do we individually have the expertise to be effective without others' input and expertise. Leaders must therefore shift from position power (top-down problem-solving and decision-making) to facilitating expert power (problem-solving and decision-making by those with the technical knowledge and understanding of the local context). They must shift their focus from micromanaging the parts to managing the interactions, connections and boundaries.

This significant shift in leadership focus and skills requires a recalibration of expectations and performance for all members of the organization—one in which the people closest to the problem are engaged and use their creativity and intellect to solve problems. And one in which the leaders create the time, space and expectations for this to happen.

Leaders facilitate individuals' engagement in the day-to-day work by promoting access to local and system information. This information includes an understanding of the goals, risks, scope, political implications and assumptions that provide the salient information needed to make good decisions. Through direction, boundary setting, mindful attention and resource allocation, organizational members become empowered and feel valued.

Encouraging diverse views and managing conflict to improve solutions and relationships also drives leadership downward. Conflict that degrades or disempowers others results in workarounds and subversive behavior. Constructive conflict, on the other hand, manifests as professional and respectful differences of opinion. Today's leaders must be skilled at conflict-utilization strategies that address the underlying support structures of unhealthy conflict, such as social hierarchies, as well as managing unhealthy individual behaviors (Scott & Pringle 2018).

Building a thinking workforce

Successful organizations of yesterday were good at execution. Execution is no longer enough. Successful organizations today are those that learn and adapt quickly in the short term while moving toward the longer-term vision. Today, we need a thinking workforce that uses knowledge and creativity to solve everyday problems.

There are two sides to the "knowledge coin"—one side focuses on knowledge sharing and the other on knowledge making, or learning. Both are critical to everyday problem-solving, ongoing improvement and adaptation (McElroy 2003). Both require time and space.

As organizational members, we're personally responsible for our own learning, regardless of the organization's contribution or commitment. We must stay current in our areas of responsibility and focus by keeping on top of professional practices, industry trends, regulatory requirements, best practices and new science or evidence. This investment in ourselves makes us much more marketable internally and externally.

As organizational leaders, we're also responsible for enabling organizational learning. This is learning that enhances the workforce's ability to effectively adapt to its circumstances. As leaders, we promote such learning through access to data and information, erring on the side of transparency and not secrecy. Access is followed by putting processes in place to bring members and information together in ways that allow for an exchange of ideas, or dialogue, giving people a chance to change the way they think. This new thinking is acknowledged by creating opportunities to explore new ways of doing business to achieve the overall goals. Through these three approaches—access, information exchange and exploration—organizational members can develop a deeper understanding of the organization's needs and adapt more readily.

Keeping it real

SUPER-LEADER PHENOMENA

A senior leadership team gathered for a weekly update meeting. Some changes had occurred, and two new super leaders would be joining the team (yes, they called them "super leaders"). As luck would have it, one of the new super leaders was able to join the group as the meeting commenced. The current team had been working on a cultural and visioning exercise that was giving them some difficulty. Super Leader #1 decided to school the team on what their vision and culture should be. It was simple for him. He couldn't imagine why they were struggling. He also had some amazing super skills, such as interrupting his new colleagues, contradicting their comments and becoming argumentative and accusatory. He engaged the team by asking, "Why would you do that?" This was his first day on the job, and he had little to no knowledge of the organization. But he, of course, was the expert. They should want his viewpoint—*not*!

Wait. It got even more entertaining. Super Leader #2 arrived in the middle of the meeting, interrupting a team member's presentation, and announced herself (at this point she certainly didn't need an introduction). The team was on the edge of their seats waiting for the inspirational message this super leader was about to impart. She gripped the table, leaned in and loudly stated that she was going to make everything better.

How, you ask? Well, because she understood how organizations were supposed to operate and had all the tools to fix the problems. She even used all the buzzwords—Six Sigma, Lean, Kaizen, etc.—you name it, it was in her super toolkit! She continued, telling the group that she was ready to make changes and wasn't afraid of anyone who might try to get in the way. Change was coming and people better be ready—or else! Inspiring.

You can imagine the sense of comfort that gave the rest of the team. The only things these super leaders lacked were red capes and tights to help them perfect their entrance and exit! This all-too-common leadership philosophy—leader as savior or superpower—is the antithesis of the leadership needed today.

WORDS MATTER

As a young nursing assistant in my first job, I was privileged to have a great RN as a mentor/teacher. She was patient and kind, and she helped me understand all the medical, technical and scientific jargon. But one day, she walked briskly out of a patient's room and told me to get a basin of water and some linens and wash up a patient who had just expired. I dutifully followed her direction while thinking about that word, *expired*, which took me to the word "perspired" and on to "messy." When I reached the bedside, I took one look at the patient and went flying out of the room. Finding the RN, I said, "She didn't expire! She's dead." Words matter. Make sure all your team members are on the same page.

LEADERSHIP THROUGH INFLUENCE

Plenty of roles in an organization can be influential even if they aren't formal leadership roles. Many, but certainly not all, of them are categorized as "support" roles and may even be viewed as less critical to the organization. This thinking couldn't be further from the truth. We were reminded of this recently when a young woman with her bachelor's degree was asked to interview for an executive assistant position. She asked us for advice on whether this was a role she should consider. The position was to support the CEO of an influential global organization. Her questions and concerns were many: 1) Is this the right path to my dream job? 2) What will I really learn to support my career path? 3) My friends think it's beneath me. Is it? and 4) My family views this as giving up on my personal goals. Am I? *Wow*—such pressure.

It was time to put old myths aside and help her understand the benefits of the opportunity: she could learn how an organization functions both administratively and operationally; improve her communication and networking skills by interfacing with all levels of the organization as well as external influencers; develop management and problem-solving skills with each daily, sometimes hourly, crisis; and most importantly, ultimately find herself operating daily in the role of "influencer," aka leader.

Fast-forward: she accepted the position, is embracing the learning opportunities outlined above and has realized that it's the journey, not the job, that makes a difference in one's development as a leader.

KNOW YOUR AUDIENCE

About one week after I started working in a leadership position at a hospital, the larger health system had a system-wide meeting. All leaders were expected to attend as some important messages were going to be delivered. They lost me at message number one. A young HR leader talked about the significant problem the organization was having with STDs. Being a clinician, I immediately thought, *Wow, they're so open about talking about sexually transmitted diseases.* This young leader continued to talk about the concern and stated that the problem was with our employees, not our patients. Now he really had my attention. I started thinking that this company had a bigger problem than STDs—what about employee confidentiality? After several more minutes of listening, I realized the STD he was talking about was "short-term disability." I immediately got the giggles and couldn't stop. I'm sure I made a big impression at that first meeting.

KEEP IT CLEAR

Two young men were in Mexico for their senior-year spring break. They wanted to go deep-sea fishing but were prone to seasickness, so Young Man #1 went to the drugstore and asked the Mexican clerk for medication for motion sickness. She provided him with his package. All the directions were in Spanish. The next morning, shortly after boarding the boat, Young Man #2 looked over to see his friend peel back the foil on a Compazine suppository, chew it up, and swallow. Right med, wrong route. Clarity matters.

✳ *Titter time: Leadership* ✳

"Due to the current workload, the light at the end of the tunnel will be turned off until further notice."
—Unknown

Self-Help

As a leader, identify the ways you keep your team engaged in terms of the following:

- Managing priorities

- Managing employee workload

- Access to information

- Keywords and messages

- Working through the paradoxes

Identify one change you could incorporate that would significantly impact your team's engagement.

_____

_____

_____

_____

_____

_____

6

Wandering Around In The Wilderness: Without A Vision, We Have No Path Forward

Have you ever been asked to be part of a "visioning" exercise for your organization? In theory, these should be robust discussions and include input from the many rather than the few. But we've all encountered the leader who tells us what the vision will be. How inspiring (cue eye roll). Here's your chance to create the energy necessary to find your true north.

The L3 Fusion Model: A journey to transformation

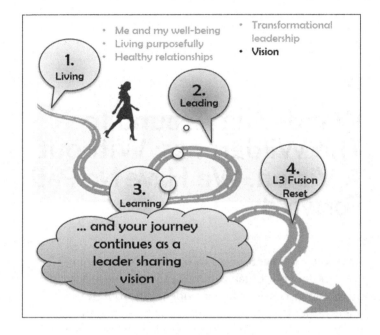

In the midst of so much new in our organizations—new leadership, new programs, new fads, new strategies, new visions, new cultures, new breakthroughs, new acquisitions, new technology, new ownership, new regulations, new expectations, new models, etc.—it's easy to get lost. And when we're lost, we're more easily discouraged, disengaged, fearful and reactive. And so are our team members. We play it safe and stick with what we know, even when there may be better ways.

Mission, vision, purpose: You won't find it on the Internet

Companies have mission statements that define their core business and objectives. These statements generally stand the test of time and provide guidance over the long haul. A vision statement is different. It provides direction during times of change while helping the organization stay true to the mission. An organization's purpose is often a combination of these two concepts—to guide its members over the long and short term. Larry Fink, CEO of BlackRock, a global investment manager, communicated this clearly in his letter (2019) to public company CEOs about purpose and profit. He stated: "Purpose is not a mere tagline or marketing campaign; it is a company's fundamental reason for being—what it does every day to create value for its shareholders. Purpose is not the sole pursuit of profits but the animating force for achieving them."

> I skate to where the puck is going to be, not where it has been.
> —Wayne Gretzky

A desirable end state, or vision, doesn't have to come from the CEO or C-suite, though. Any leader can and should have a vision for their area of responsibility—one that's big, inspiring, shared and communicated over and over again. This end state is what we aspire to be, such as "the best in class," and/or what we desire to accomplish through a change initiative, such as "save 1,000 lives from harm." Vision connects the dots from our daily work to a desired end state, helping us move forward with a steady determination: #OhThePlacesWeCanGo.

A vision is powerful when it's shared by the organization's members and offers a sense of direction. It drives the organization's time, conversations, resources and decisions. When the vision is shared, it provides meaningful connections to the members' daily activities and contributions and instills a sense of pride and meaning. The best leaders understand that their key task is inspiring a shared vision, not selling their own idiosyncratic view of the world.

The status is not quo

Often, a vision is counter to the current state or dominant culture and projects a positive alternative. It doesn't mire us in past abuses or old ways. And it doesn't just appeal to our reason or logic. Rather, it also appeals to our humanness, our emotions, and propels us forward. Because change and innovation are passionate processes, it's important to pay attention to the emotional part of the organization. We've all invested in the status quo—it's familiar and requires less effort than changing the way we do our business. Going through a change involves giving up arrangements in which considerable energy and time have been invested (Poole 2004). Successful planned change requires a commitment grounded in an engaging vision and deep emotional involvement with the program.

Connecting our purpose, or inner truth, to an engaging vision for the organization creates personal energy! When leaders take the time to communicate and connect the work to a vision that inspires others, it becomes shared. And this shared vision creates collective energy at the operational level. We get much more engaged when we see and understand how our work contributes to something big and important.

Keeping it real

CREATING A SHARED VISION

We were working with a healthcare organization that was having trouble getting its people on board with an initiative that involved changing the way they delivered care to people with mental illnesses in their community. With just a little prompting, the director was able to articulate the "why" behind the change, which was quite inspiring! We then did an exercise in which several small groups from her team constructed vision statements for a broader group tied to this work. The rest of the room judged these statements. The first three statements were met with loud boos and thumbs down. But the room exploded with applause for the fourth one, and multiple people said that this was a cause they'd invest in. The message spoke to both the head and the heart. They were able to connect the dots between the need for the change and the organization's vision in a way that inspired and energized others to get involved.

CONNECTING THE DOTS

Quite often individuals produce data (lots of data) but don't know how it's used or why it's useful to management. Right here is Leadership Failure 101. But moving on.

A CEO expressed that his overall vision for the organization was to remove a long-established structural deficit and provide transparency to internal and external parties throughout the process. Sounds boring, but certainly important. So how do you inspire an accounting team to get behind this vision and realize that they can be impactful?

They assumed it was just a scorekeeping exercise when really, it was a learning opportunity for them as well. Historically, the accounting team thought only about the tasks they performed every day to produce the numbers. The question "What do people do with your data?" was met with blank stares from the team. They knew that someone pulled all the data together and it ended up in the financial statements. Their job was simply to produce a number. Little did they realize how critical their numbers were to telling the story of the organization's financial health.

When we took our time and helped the accountants understand the critical role each of them and their respective entries played in providing management, banks, investors, etc. with information that was accurate, timely and informative, their attitude turned around. They were more productive and engaged. And over time, they became more inquisitive.

THE ACCOUNTING TEAM'S VISION

The unspoken vision was "We produce numbers." But after going through this process, their spoken and regularly communicated vision became "We provide vital and actionable information about the health of our organization to our team."

The journey continued. Once we showed them how to take the data and format it in a way that everyone could understand, they were inspired to communicate what they were seeing to others in the organization. They were eager to help their colleagues better understand the financial results and how their unit goals could impact the overall vision of lowering the deficit and becoming more transparent. The transparency became easy—they were proud of their work and wanted to be part of that sharing process.

There are rules for posting and sharing financial data, but many companies share only what's necessary. When you make the story informative, relatable and available (while of course still following the regulated guidelines), getting commitment to a goal is much easier.

The whole team, not just the CFO or CEO, now has a sense of ownership. They value their contribution and know that insiders and outsiders also value their contribution. The accountants' excitement was contagious and carried over to other functional and operational units. Everyone was part of the success—not just the few at the top.

Such is the power of an inspiring shared vision!

✴ *Titter time: Vision* ✴

"People often say that motivation doesn't last. Well, neither does bathing—that's why we recommend it daily."
—Zig Ziglar

 Self-Help

Ask yourself, "Whom do I want to work with? How do these statements make me feel?"

Vision Statements

	UGH! Boring!		Count me in!!!
Example 1: Accounting Department	We produce numbers	vs.	We provide vital and actionable information about the health of our organization to our team.
Example 2: Nursing Department	We deliver excellent patient care	vs.	We respect each of our patients and treat them like family, keeping them safe, informed and cared for.
Example 3: Change Initiative	We will implement and document in the electronic medical record	vs.	We are creating one source of truth for our patients and caregivers to promote first class care.

- Now it's your turn. Create a vision for your team that's inspiring and that you think will connect their heads and their hearts to a desired future state.

_____

_____

_____

- Ask your team what they think about this vision. What would they change? Can they embrace it? Is it a stretch? Will it contribute in a significant way to the organization's mission? Can they see themselves in this future state? How could they contribute to it? What do they need to walk this talk?

_____

_____

_____

_____

7

Fifty Shades Of Culture: If You Can't Define It, You Can't Change It

Chances are you've experienced *Groundhog Day* moments. We certainly have! Eager to discuss an organization's culture with its management team one day, we were greeted with silence. Not one person could define what that culture was—or at least they weren't willing to share that definition in an open forum. We could sense a general fear, as the leader believed and mandated that they all existed in "happy land." At the next meeting, this leader wasn't present, and we had an engaged discussion about the culture and how it could be more inclusive and inspiring. Fast-forward to the next meeting. Yep, you guessed it—Groundhog Day! The executive was present, and his beady eyes circled the room, challenging anyone to bring up something contrary to his beliefs. So disappointing and limiting for the team and the organization.

The L3 Fusion Model:
A journey to transformation

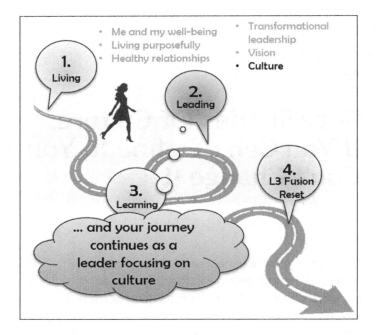

We often think of culture as a mysterious, undefined force that impacts our organizations in both positive and negative ways. As long as this force is allowed to remain mysterious and gray, it will continue to affect many aspects of everyday organizational life, including (1) how power is demonstrated and used, (2) how the work gets done, (3) how emotions are displayed, and (4) how decisions are made and by whom. It's therefore critical to unveil the mystery of culture, particularly when change is needed.

Culture is how a group of people, such as an organization, department or family, behaves collectively. While we all have personal beliefs and values, we don't always act on them in the workplace. We may hold ourselves back out of fear or respect or because of other constraints. Individuals act on expectations they believe are in their own best interests within that setting. These collective actions become "the way we do things around here": the culture.

Cultures are created over time and can be enabling or disabling forces in times of change. Cultural health is similar to human health. We can look healthy on the outside but have a life-changing disease. The earlier we identify the symptoms, the greater the possibility of curing the illness. The longer the illness goes on, the more difficult the cure. When we have built-in practices that promote resilience, we're able to recover more quickly from setbacks.

Organizations, too, can become ill and decline, stumble and fall. Their decline is self-inflicted most of the time but can also result from rapid and unforeseen change, such as an environmental disaster. Recovery from the more common, self-inflicted cases is possible and largely within the leadership's control. But this recovery requires diagnosing problems in new ways and addressing them aggressively. It begins with an understanding of the organization's current state of affairs.

This understanding includes a diagnosis of the primary culture and the subcultures—the pockets of culture that define a specific group, profession or department. Subcultures can aid or interfere with the desired overall culture. For example, groups of lawyers, engineers, physicians or nurses may have their own sets of shared values, norms and perceptions that differ from those of other groups in the organization and that impact the overall organization in positive or negative ways.

Organizational introspection becomes a critical survival exercise during a change or crisis. It requires reframing the organization in ways that help create a better sense of the situation and opportunities. It often begins with identifying a "transcendent culture" to achieve a "higher calling." The higher calling is clearly called out, as well as new expectations and behaviors to support the calling. The patient-safety movement in healthcare is a good example of creating a transcendent culture. It's not about professionals and workers focusing on their own interests—rather, the movement is an attempt to ensure that the collective values and behaviors are those that promote reliable operations and minimize errors to keep patients safe. The expectation is that the safety of patients takes priority over professional autonomy and organizational efficiency. When these new expectations are supported through new structures, the culture begins to shift.

Cultural revelation

Many different types of cultures are found in organizations today, and these cultures end up defining the organization. Different cultures produce different dynamics and outcomes. Several common types are identified below.

- **Power culture**—A power culture is based on a single, centralized source of power and decision-making. Organizations with power cultures are often small and entrepreneurial or in crisis mode. Because of its top-down direction and focus, a power culture can respond quickly when there are high stakes and short timelines. But it doesn't leverage the knowledge of the larger team or make the best use of organizational resources.

- **Role culture**—A role culture operates through its functional components with a focus on rank and status. Think "big government." Job descriptions are the foundation of work. Power comes with position and the entire organization is rule-bound and conservative, with most individuals protecting their jobs and power. Knowledge is power and tends to be hoarded and protected by managers and function experts. Learning is only for new employees and those seeking promotions. Creativity isn't encouraged and threatens the status quo. Decisions are hierarchical. Change is difficult.

- **Person culture**—In a person culture, the individuals (leaders or employees) are put first, with everything else providing support. Often, the executive team acts as if the organization is their club and exists for their aggrandizement rather than for their customers and/or core purpose. Mission takes a back seat. Respect for the individual becomes entitlement for the many or few—this could mean lifetime employment simply by virtue of having been hired. There's little or no overall cohesion throughout the organization. It's a collection of individuals who band together to make it easier for each person to do their own thing (a group rather than a team). This culture isn't capable of performing as needed in a turbulent environment.

- **Task culture**—In a task culture, people are focused on each task or project. The goal is to get the job done by bringing together the appropriate resources and the right people at the right level of the organization. It's a team culture, and the team's work tends to overpower individual objectives, status and styles. The matrix organization is a modern implementation of the task culture. It works well in a growing and low-to-medium-risk environment. It's often promoted for product development and program acquisition. But during tough times or rapid change, flexibility and sustainability become problematic due to lack of structures and social attributes needed to sustain cohesion.

- **Action culture**—An action culture focuses on disciplined contribution to the organization's overall goals. Every member is considered important and intelligent and expected to take the right action at the right place and time. These actions are supported by performance standards, values and accountabilities. Leadership is distributed and focuses on assuring that members have the knowledge and resources they need to take the appropriate actions. Self-organization is encouraged. Leaders ensure multidirectional collaboration with line-of-site activity consistent with the organization's objectives. An action culture is critical in organizations and industries going through tremendous change, such as healthcare, banking and education.

Each type of culture is perpetuated by the healthy and dysfunctional behaviors within them. As leaders and members, each of us is responsible for understanding how our behaviors and activities influence the experiences of others. When we change our own approach, rather than impose our way on others, we begin to see the creative forces move culture in a new direction: #ElevateYourCulture.

Time to make amazing happen

There are many perpetuators of culture in the workplace. We'll focus on a few negative behavioral patterns that are critical for leaders to diagnose and
mitigate, as well as some leadership practices that,
when done well, perpetuate the desired culture.

Behavioral patterns in organizations are supported by
the system's social hierarchies and underlying structures. To change the behavioral patterns, we must

address the structures that support them. As a personal example, when we want to change our unhealthy eating habits, we also have to change the way we grocery shop. Rather than buy whatever looks good at the time, we create a menu of healthy options and shop from that list. This is a structural change that supports, hopefully, a behavioral change. When the chips and salsa aren't in the house, there's less opportunity for us to binge! Similarly, when the social hierarchies in organizations allow bad behaviors from a select few with strong financial or political influence, the pattern continues. When these behaviors are consistently addressed through a thoughtful change in the performance-measurement process (a structural change), the behavioral pattern will change as well.

Three particularly prevalent and destructive patterns of behavior that plague organizations today are described below. These patterns perpetuate unhealthy cultures that suck the life out of the members and misdirect time, energy and resources.

- **Normalization of deviance**—This is when the social hierarchies allow behaviors that are self-serving. The needs of the whole are subverted in favor of personal needs (such as protection, power and influence). These behaviors often include breaking the rules, and this behavior may be exhibited by anywhere from one person or group to multiple individuals or groups. Breaking the rules then becomes the norm, which is continuously reinforced by no immediate negative consequences. In fact, there are positive consequences for the rule breakers—they're able to act more freely without the encumbrances that rules impose.

- **Passive-aggressive "nice"**—This is the general tendency in an organization to remain silent to "preserve relationships" rather than address the issues and seek new solutions. As a result, the members don't speak openly about the elephant in the room. Instead, the elephant is discussed in the hallways, after the meeting and in secret e-mails and texts. And the fundamental problems continue unaddressed.

- **Denial and blame**—In *How the Mighty Fall* (2009), Jim Collins describes the dynamics of leaders and teams on their way down. As they move through the cycle of denial (denial of risk and peril), they avoid sharing the grim facts or harsh realities. They often assert strong opinions but without supporting evidence. They shy away from debate. And rather than learn from their painful experiences, they often focus on whom to blame. Blame becomes the norm for their failures.

Each of us needs a toolkit to help create and perpetuate the positive attributes needed in today's workplaces. Rituals and ceremonies are two powerful tools in this kit. They can be used to perpetuate stability or promote meaningful change.

Personal rituals—such as a morning Starbucks drink (one of us embraces this ritual religiously), meditation, a morning run (or walk) and a weekly happy-hour gathering with friends—can anchor us in the midst of unpredictability. Likewise, traditional celebrations, such as graduations, religious holidays, birthdays and an annual weekend with old friends, also bring stability and order to our lives.

In the same way, organizational rituals and celebrations communicate the company's identity, delineate key relationships, transmit values and contribute to the culture. When these activities are purposefully altered, leaders signal meaningful change and a new direction. Such organizational rituals and celebrations include activities that celebrate new products and achievements, induction ceremonies, new-hire and/or retirement festivities, project pranks, storytelling, accomplishment-recognition methods and employee-of-the month celebrations. When properly conducted, they can fire up enthusiasm and deepen commitment. When done poorly and/or disingenuously, they become cold and empty forms that people resent, ridicule and avoid.

Leaders must use their tools wisely and thoughtfully. For example, have you ever been asked to take part in a retreat that was completely for the leader's benefit? This individual was so excited to have people come to their beach house and play games to promote "teamwork," but it became an exercise in "all about me" and not "all about you." Instead of enjoying a great day at the beach with co-workers, everyone was wishing that a giant wave would carry that leader off to a different shore.

Never waste a good crisis

There's no better time to get the organization's attention than when there's an impending external threat. These threats come in many forms—a new competitor with power and resources, for example, or significant organizational failures such as large financial losses, poor publicly reported quality, fraudulent practices or security breaches. These threats are significant at the system level and can also affect members on a personal level—reputation, financial security, emotional stability, future opportunities, etc.

Crises are a crucial leadership test and, rightfully, impact a leader's credibility. A crisis creates a moment in history in which the decisions and actions taken bend the organization's trajectory positively or negatively. It's a time people will look back to—and they'll assess the success or failure of the leadership of that time.

During a crisis, it's critical to motivate and engage the organization's members to be part of the solution. This requires transparency and clarity around the crisis itself. Relevant information must be disseminated and there needs to be an open dialogue about the surrounding circumstances and missed opportunities. The focus should be on strategies, values and expectations—not people. Leaders have the opportunity to rally the team around a common vision and transcendent culture that moves the organization forward. Never waste a good crisis!

Keeping it real

THE TALE OF TWO CEOS

We worked with two CEOs who each faced a crisis in their organization. One responded as a mature leader. The other, simply put, behaved badly. In each case, the organization's trajectory was impacted significantly by their actions.

CEO #1 led an organization in a competitive market. She continuously stated that to stay relevant, they would need to become the "innovation leader" in their market. This vision was communicated over and over again, and yet they found themselves struggling in this space and asked for our help. We observed a pattern of behavior that was getting in the way—leaders at all levels below the CEO wouldn't speak up. They wouldn't ask questions in meetings, agree or disagree with the leader, share new ideas or give their opinions.

We decided to dig a bit deeper. We soon discovered another pattern of behavior—three senior executives routinely behaved badly in the leadership team meetings, even when guests were present. Their subtle and not-so-subtle forms of disrespect included inattention during presentations (looking at their phones or having side conversations). They would openly snicker when someone struggled with a question or concept, and they would make comments under their breath about people's physical appearance. We also discovered that some senior leaders had attempted to counsel the group to modify their behavior but ended up being ostracized. The message to the organization was loud and clear and traveled like wildfire: you and your contributions aren't valued or needed.

We recommended some new ways of conducting business, which included changing behavioral expectations and making structural shifts that would incentivize innovation and decrease risks to the innovators. The CEO agreed to the change. She would not, however, change her ways or accept personal coaching.

In this scenario, the CEO made it perfectly clear that she had no intention of changing the behaviors getting in the way of creating an innovative culture. The innovators became further disillusioned and left, and the organization fell further and further behind.

CEO #2 shared with us a story about a crisis in her organization: the entire emergency department (ED) staff threatened to walk out and strike. This was one of the largest EDs in the state, and they cared for some of the most complex patients. The staff (physicians, nurses and technicians) had had enough. They felt that their safety concerns, which they'd tried to communicate over a two-year period, weren't being addressed. They were past the point of threatening a walkout—they were actively planning it.

When the CEO realized what was going on, she became personally involved at every level. She met with multiple teams and asked about their specific concerns. She listened. She didn't throw anyone under the bus. In fact, she brought the management team along with her on this journey. She said out loud to employees, management and providers, "I have failed you. Your issues are real and long standing. I'm sorry that it took so long to hear you, but you have my full attention now." Together, they put together a plan of correction and a communication structure that included daily leadership rounding in the ED. They worked the plan until the issues were resolved. The ED staff became this CEO's biggest fans. They forgave her. They supported her. They appreciated her attention, frank talking and willingness to own up to the situation.

The CEO described this as a cultural crisis not just for the ED but the entire organization. This crisis sparked a disciplined journey toward a new vision of engagement—the engagement of the people who did the work. This CEO changed the culture over time through her unrelenting focus on new expectations. This leader was successful because she allowed herself to be vulnerable to the team.

THE POWER OF VUNERABILITY

We also worked with a leader who had trouble inspiring her team. This individual knew her personal communication challenges, so a facilitator was hired to assist with a team-building exercise. The facilitator asked this leader to encourage her team to do something, but to do so in a "ridiculous and made-up language." To the leader's surprise, the team got completely involved in the exercise. They were amused by her willingness to be vulnerable, engaging and funny.

Would the team be able to figure out the message being conveyed? It really didn't matter—it was the journey they were on together that was adding the value. When the team building was in full swing, the group realized that a meaningful transformation was occurring with their participation. Going forward, they were committed—committed to working with leadership in setting goals, to supporting each other to reach those goals and to entertaining new perspectives if a redirection was necessary.

Years later, some of these team members still speak enthusiastically about that day and how it changed their view of leadership and culture. They took what they learned and modeled their own leadership skills to support that vulnerability and openness to change. *Wow*—now that's something to celebrate!

✳ *Titter time: Culture* ✳

"The past, the present and the future walked into a bar. It was tense."
—Unknown

Self-Help

Think about how you can contribute in ways that help you and others stay enthusiastically focused on the right things. Start small. Be authentic.

- Refer to the culture types identified above and describe the culture (values, beliefs, expectations) of your organization in your own words.

  _____

  _____

  _____

  _____

- Describe any destructive patterns of behavior you observe that get in the way of success.

  _____

  _____

  _____

  _____

- Identify ways that you can personally influence this pattern in a positive way.

   _____

   _____

   _____

   _____

8

In My Defense, I Was Left Unsupervised: Leaders Facilitate The Work Of Teams

A team or task force can be effective, or it can resemble a soccer field of five-year-olds chasing a ball with no clear intent to get it across the goal line. The players are adorable and giving it their best effort, running after the ball and often kicking it in the wrong direction. The coach is aghast. They smile at him when he delivers his expert knowledge on how to score that winning goal, but they don't listen to a word he says. They're contributing and having fun, though!

Recently, we participated in a similar exercise. A leader had an affinity for her supposed structure for a process. There were many participants on this task force, and when asked to present their ideas, they rushed to the wall with their multicolored sticky notes and flip charts. Not one person had a clue about how to reach the necessary outcome, but they sure loved participating— until the end of the session, when they realized they were no further along than when they'd walked in the room.

Equally concerning: Have you ever been on a team where you felt as if you were entering a war zone and had to buckle down your helmet, take a swig of bourbon and draw your weapon before carefully entering the room? Yes—teams can be challenging.

The L3 Fusion Model: A journey to transformation

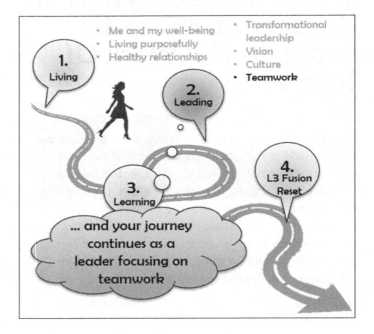

We spend a large amount of our time working, or playing, on teams. These teams may stretch across multiple shifts, departments and even organizations. Team memberships connect us to people with whom we have established relationships, as well as people who are mostly unknown to us.

A team is more than a group of people coming together to work or play, though. A team comes together for a purpose. Ideally:

- A team has a small number of people with complementary skills

- Its members are committed to a common purpose

- There's a known set of performance goals

- Its members take an approach to which they hold themselves mutually accountable

The benefits of effective teamwork are well documented: enhanced effectiveness, improved efficiency, lower stress and more client satisfaction. But the literature also shows that organizations aren't getting the performances they need and desire from their teams. With so many complex and difficult issues in the workplace, and with the significant assets that strong teams can bring, it's a strategic imperative to achieve value from teamwork.

Because we rely on each other for information, skills and activities in today's workplaces, a team is often a good structural choice when it comes to getting the work done. Teams can be created and dissolved as needed. They facilitate boundary crossing and breaking down silos (Casciaro, Edmondson & Jang

2019). Teams have more knowledge and diversity of perspective than an individual and can promote buy-in to a plan or solution more quickly.

Teams also run the risk of succumbing to failure, stagnating from lack of purpose and progress or disintegrating because of personal agendas, social pressures and conflicts. It can be difficult to manage the gaps and tensions that teams often experience.

Trust is an important ingredient for fully optimizing a team. Without trust, members seek to protect their immediate interests, to the detriment of the entire system's long-term effectiveness and well-being. Teams and team members have values or principles that guide their behaviour, often without their awareness. They also have daily norms at a more superficial level. When a team shares values and takes action collectively, a sense of group identity that propels the work forward is developed. Otherwise, the opposite often occurs—the team stalls. They cannot resolve their conflicts or agree on the way forward, so their work dies a slow death.

Commitment to the team's work over the team members is important. If there isn't a focus on the work, or purpose, dysfunctional actions and behaviors will occur, and they'll feed the system's underlying problems and allow the status quo to continue. A commitment to people over purpose can be impacted by social norms and hierarchies that are already in existence, such as "passive-aggressive nice," fear of rocking the boat or top-down decision-making.

In many organizations, social hierarchies become power structures that affect team conflict, collaboration and decision-making. Healthcare organizations, in particular, have unique social hierarchies. The dominance of specific professions, such as management and medicine, impact day-to-day dynamics—dynamics such as communication practices, conflict, collaboration and displays of emotions. Team members will often defer to the person with the most perceived power, whether or not they have the expertise and/or knowledge needed for the situation. For example, physicians' opinions often go unchallenged in healthcare organizations even when they opine on practices that go beyond their education and expertise. Organizational members, rather than confront or conflict, often choose to remain silent or acquiesce to the physician, taking on the role of a victim. It's important to unearth the organization's norms, values, expectations and assumptions when progress stalls. The team's communication and conflict strategies must deal with the underlying power and decision-making structures that protect the current state. Otherwise, there will be plenty of activity by plenty of people, but the fundamental problems won't be addressed and the outcomes won't change.

We discuss three common failures in regards to teamwork and strategies to address them. The common failures center around purpose, diversity and team management.

- Purpose—The purpose of the team isn't clear and/or the team members aren't clear about why they're on the team.

- Diversity—The team isn't diverse or inclusive enough to tap the thinking and perspectives needed to solve the problem or meet the goals.

- Team management—Leaders don't know how to manage the diversity of styles, interests and norms within a team.

Purpose—you get three guesses

Have you ever been invited (or summoned) to participate on a team whose purpose you were unclear about? Or worse yet, maybe you attended a team meeting or two and still weren't clear on it. Unfortunately, this isn't uncommon. As team members, each of us needs to understand why we're coming together—we must understand what the team is expected to accomplish and why (the team purpose).

Connect your "why" to your "what"

It's also important to understand why you specifically were invited to participate. Are you representing a specific group or perspective? Is it a work style you bring to the group (are you an innovator, a driver of decisions, a detail-oriented person who understands the status quo, an integrator who's able to bring people together)? Is it because of your role in the organization and the impact of this work on that role? Or is it because you're a subject-matter expert?

Team members may be recruited for a variety of reasons, and when these reasons are shared with the group, not only are individuals affirmed for the strengths they bring, but the playing field is leveled, minimizing the impact of social hierarchies and norms that get in the way of open dialogue and problem-solving.

Diversity promotes insight

Complex problem-solving requires diverse viewpoints. Too often we see the same people recruited to participate on teams. Often they're chosen because of their titles or interpersonal style. Teams fail because leaders don't effectively incorporate diverse work styles and perspectives into their teams. As a result, great ideas go unheard or unrealized and performance suffers.

Diversity supports a team's competitive advantage. Research identifies four diverse work styles that bring useful perspectives and approaches to teamwork (Johnson, Christfort & Christfort 2017)—the work of generating ideas, making decisions and solving problems. Each of us is a composite of these four styles but more closely aligned with one or two. When assembling a team, consider a balance of individuals who demonstrate these styles:

- Pioneers—the risk-takers who value possibilities, focus on the big picture and are drawn to bold new ideas

- Guardians—the pragmatists who value stability and bring order and rigor, data and facts and lessons from the past

- Drivers—the results-oriented people who value a challenge and bring logic, data and momentum

- Integrators—the relationship-focused people who draw the team together, are diplomatic and are focused on consensus

When assembling a team, also consider individuals' internal expertise and knowledge, industry expertise and experience, political insights, personal interests and willingness to learn and participate.

Diverse styles, skills and perspectives bring different strengths to the team but can also create tension and conflict. That's perfectly okay, and expected, but the tension and conflict must be actively managed.

Go team!

Whether you're leading the team or you're a team member, be prepared. Everyone has something to contribute to the game, so don't waste others' time or opportunities by dropping in without practice or preparation: #SuitUpForTheTeam.

And while you're at it, make it fun—after all, many of us spend most of our time at work. Effective teams balance seriousness with humor and play. Joking and playful banter are essential sources of creativity and team spirit. Humor releases tension and helps resolve issues that arise from both day-to-day routines and emergencies.

Leaders need to create the space and time for teams to come together. There's nothing more disheartening than being recruited to participate only to be told you can't be released from your other work responsibilities during the meeting time. As leaders of team members, we must find creative ways to help them participate, contribute and be engaged in the work.

Teams also need a leader to manage the team itself. This leadership requires the ability to actively manage the group's diversity and conflicts, keep the team engaged and achieve the end goals. Here are some practical recommendations for managing a team.

- Have an executive sponsor—A higher-level champion, or executive sponsor, provides clarity and guidance about the purpose of the team's work. This person is kept apprised of the group's progress and helps remove barriers, provides resources and shares their insights as needed.

- Develop a team charter—Create a clear, succinct document that outlines the team's purpose, goals, scope, timelines, authority and membership. Share this document at the first meeting and ask for feedback. Also share your thoughts with the team on the strengths that each member brings to the group.

- Use an agenda—Create a timed agenda and send it out at least twenty-four hours before the meeting. Be clear about the purpose of each meeting and avoid the time-consuming mistake of having everyone report. Rather, ask for updates to be sent out ahead of time with the agenda. The meeting agenda should focus on problem-solving and/or decision-making that keeps the team moving toward its goals.

- Manage the group—Share expectations in the beginning. Come prepared with questions to draw out the members' best thinking. Encourage the team to dive more deeply into specific issues and express related ideas and experiences. Leading with curiosity and inquiry encourages diverse thoughts and ideas and promotes psychological safety (Casciaro, Edmondson & Jang 2019). Encourage constructive conflict and ask the group members to hold each other accountable for respectful conversations and disagreements. Inject humor and make it fun! Draw out the introverts and set limits on the extroverts when needed. Stick to the meeting timeline—start and end on time—and allow time between meetings for work that's more conducive to individuals. Some tasks are better done outside the meeting room. Hold the team accountable for their assignments and deliverables.

- Write a meeting summary—Create a meeting summary that identifies (1) attendees, (2) decisions made, (3) assignments and timelines and (4) next steps. Send this out to the group within twenty-four hours (ideally) of the meeting's end.

- Communicate up—Provide the executive sponsor with progress reports. Share barriers that can't be overcome or additional resource needs.

- Celebrate progress—Create symbolic rituals and ceremonies to define and celebrate special achievements along the way.

If you're struggling to facilitate the team, consider recruiting a co-leader with complementary skills. Also, find a coach for, and additional training related to, team facilitation and change management.

 ## Keeping it real

KEEP IT FUN

Dr. Seuss says in *The Cat in the Hat*, 'I know it is wet and the sun is not sunny, but we can have lots of good fun that is funny.' Yes, we can! Life is short and we need to enjoy it. Don't just focus single-mindedly on the task at hand, shunning non-work-related discussion. Encourage people to keep it real and enjoy themselves and each other. At times, it may stretch the boundaries of good taste—go with it. Just remember, self-deprecating comments work; personal attacks don't!

Part of the fun is celebrating along the way. Get creative about special and symbolic ways to connect their contributions to advancing the bigger goals. Recruit a fun person to focus specifically on this. One of my favorite celebrations was when a talented team member put a hilarious message about the group's accomplishments (specifically, creating a standard of care around chronic kidney disease) to music and invited a colleague to sing the message while he played an accordion. Hilarious! Fun! Team members felt valued. And it was much easier to recruit for the next standard-of-care team.

BE A GOOD TEAM PLAYER AND DON'T BURN YOUR BRIDGES

Never fall into the "I thought they knew" trap. Come on—put on those big-girl pants and be confident in what you have to contribute.

Ask yourself: "What does it mean to be a good team player?" and "How do I address rogue team members who have a negative presence/view?"

Leaders work to minimize a team's weaknesses and maximize its strengths. Put people on the team with skills and attributes that will help ensure success, but be willing to move team members around if you see they can be utilized in a different role within the team. You might do so often, especially as a project evolves. Rogue team players are individuals who don't want to contribute to the working sessions. They undermine or throw out negative (not constructive) feedback, try to dominate the discussions and aren't supportive of getting to the end result. Manage them to a better place or off the team.

Great teams will form lasting relationships, which may even continue after you've left the team or the company. These individuals will always be willing to help you should you need advice, networking, etc.

Do you view yourself as a leader? How do you lead your team(s)? How do you define success? Leadership is hard— it calls on skills that we may not excel in. Not all leaders are understanding, motivational, authentic, etc. But when we're open to learning the how of leadership, it will soon become part of our framework. It's also important to surround ourselves with individuals who have mastered these skills and can bridge our gap in learning.

Our humanness complicates everything. But it also makes what we do and how we do it more important and meaningful. We must never lose perspective regarding what it means to be an employee at all levels in the organization. When we as leaders become disconnected from reality, we pose unnecessary challenges to our staff and they begin to lose trust in the management team. Be fearless! Be supportive! Your team will notice.

RESPECT

Respect and involvement go a long way. Consider the golden rule. Respectful behavior is at the root of it. As far as being involved—how many times has a decision been made about something in your area of expertise without your being consulted? It feels pretty crappy. Well, the same thing goes for those on our team. We must be smart enough to appropriately involve folks who have specific knowledge in important decisions. That also means we need to know who has this knowledge. Let's make a practice of finding them and working with them.

CONNECT YOUR WHY TO YOUR WHAT

It doesn't take a rocket scientist to get this one. Whenever we communicate a what we need to include a why. We've wanted to know "why" since we were kids, and this holds true today, no matter how old we are— connect your why to your what.

Titter time: Teamwork

"One team member said to another after a tough meeting: 'You're an a**hole.' When ordered by her supervisor to apologize to the person she had insulted, she said: 'I'm sorry you're such an a**hole.'"
—Adapted from David Peck in Tracy
 Kidder's *Soul of a New Machine*,
 1981

 Self-Help

Consider a time when you were part of a team that accomplished great things and left you feeling energized. Now reflect on these questions:

• What made this such a good experience?

_____

_____

_____

_____

- How did the team's leadership, membership, interactions, accomplishments and struggles affect your experience?

  _____

  _____

  _____

  _____

- What strengths did you contribute to the team?

  _____

  _____

  _____

  _____

- What can you take away from this experience to strengthen teamwork in your areas of influence?

  _____

  _____

  _____

  _____

9

Herding Cats: Structures Keep Us On Track

A new leader is in town, and your hopes of nirvana and a new way of thinking have just been doused. His first communication on the "new structure" is a flop. The rollout is even more of a fiasco. The messaging lacks clarity, direction, rationale, inclusiveness and enthusiasm. In the hallways and break rooms, everyone is talking about what this new structure means for them. Stories are becoming epic. The "list" (who's going first and which businesses will be eliminated) is being developed. The end is near! Some of your colleagues articulate a balanced viewpoint, some are full of doom and gloom, some have no filters but are saying exactly what you're thinking and some are just plain angry! Don't you wish you could create a new episode of *The Office*? This leader's emotional incompetence and lack of structural know-how would be perfect fodder. Pick your title: "The Flop," "Dumber than Cat Crap," or "Circling the Drain."

The L3 Fusion Model:
A journey to transformation

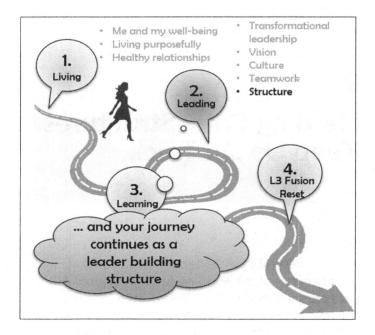

Disruptive innovation is changing all the rules for today's organizations. There are significantly more external demands coming at an accelerated tempo. Ultimately, these demands require serving our customers in better ways, whether through more effective operations, mass customization or new offerings (Morlinghaus 2019). They call for an expansion of internal capabilities to compete on entirely new terms. In the absence of clear, workable structures, the effectiveness of highly dedicated and skilled employees becomes seriously impaired. New structures are needed to provide direction and harness the energy and intelligence of all the members, not just a select few. Warning—this chapter is not for the faint of heart!

The organizational structure is the engine that drives performance. It's intended to organize the people side of the business. It determines how things get done—how the work is allocated and coordinated. Structure dictates the relationship of roles and defines the mechanisms for formal communication and decision-making functions. It establishes the boundaries of acceptable behaviors through the design of positions and responsibilities, authority, incentives and disincentives, technology and a variety of controls within the organization. Technology is an increasingly important component of structure as it can connect formerly siloed activities that impact customers and outcomes.

Organizational spirit is also impacted by structure. Think about the intangible qualities of start-up companies. There's a deep sense of connection and mutual purpose. Engagement is high. (Let's not confuse this with a Rocky-Mountain high!) There's an intense commitment to the business's purpose, the customers' needs and the employees' experiences. But often as the organization grows and becomes more complex, the structure expands and the spirit wanes. It's possible, though, to find a middle ground in which dynamic companies can add structure and discipline while still retaining deep engagement and meaning (Gulati 2019).

Structures for the new world

Today's organizations must be flexible, adaptable, innovative and capable of rapidly responding to internal and external unknowns. At the same time, they must be reliable and have enough cohesion to keep everyone going in the same direction.

High-risk organizations and industries, such as healthcare, aviation, aeronautics and nuclear power, are particularly challenging. They have unique structural needs. Errors can lead to loss of life or body function. The organizations are opaque, with many subsystems of specialists and services dependent on each other for information. These subsystems are often not well understood by planners, leaders or patient-care providers, and they require rapid decisions in situations where individuals and groups are unstable, personally threatened or threatening to others.

Reliability is the quality of yielding the desired results repeatedly and consistently. Adaptability is the quality of being able to adjust to new conditions. To achieve both adaptability and reliability in today's complex and high-risk organizations, there must be the right balance of risk management and innovation. This balance occurs through the design of the following:

- Decision-making structures (hierarchical, matrix, horizontal)
- Tight and loose controls
- Structural coordination and integration

These are described in more detail below.

Top-down and tight

Top-down (hierarchical) leadership structures are intended to maintain authority and accountability for organizational goals. Decision-making is concentrated at the top (see image below). These structures are also referred to as command-and-control structures, and for good reason. Tight controls are put in place to promote standardized practices that reduce organizational risks. These tight controls, to be effective, are accompanied by leadership's buy-in to consistently address breaches of these tight controls when workarounds or unethical practices occur. Leaders set explicit boundaries between acceptable and unacceptable practices, as well as through fair and equitable follow-up and punishment when these boundaries aren't adhered to (Healy & Serafeim 2019). When leaders turn the other way or play favorites, punishing some but not others, tight controls become a farce and an impediment.

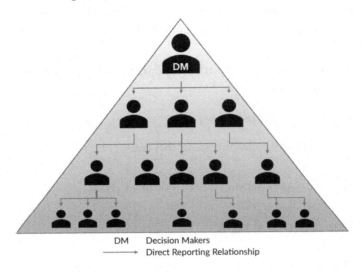

DM   Decision Makers
⟶   Direct Reporting Relationship

Top-Down (Hierarchical) Organizational Structure

A command-and-control environment can be effective, but only when the stakes are high and the timeline is short. Think about firefighters during an out-of-control blaze—not the time for debate and consensus. Or consider a surgeon operating in the OR. In the surgical environment, the doctor rules with little question or justification. She has the expertise and skills to operate safely and effectively. She calls the shots. *But* remove her from that setting and place her in another—such as a CEO position—and things begin to deteriorate. This person is no expert in corporate governance, nor has she necessarily developed the skills to work collaboratively or build consensus. When she acts in the boardroom as she does in the operating room, it all goes downhill. Her team feels disempowered and isolated. And when she uses back channels to discuss matters with those she knows, instead of those with the expertise, she makes decisions that can hurt the organization. Unfortunately, this happens too often. Leaders take an approach that works in one setting and try to use it in all settings. In their defense, command and control has worked well in many settings over the past fifty years, but it falls apart when more expertise, knowledge and diverse points of view are needed to respond to the complexity. The consequences of leading in antiquated ways go beyond being wrong—the destruction is significant! People become demoralized and walk, or they're laid off through downsizing and service eliminations.

That said, certain tight controls are important. The finance function, for example, incorporates an authority matrix for spending limits to decrease risky and unnecessary spending. The oversight is designed to prevent spending beyond one's authority, span of control and level of competence. In the information systems function, there are necessary tight controls around security and privacy of information. Likewise, an organization's internal audit function provides tighter oversight of regulatory compliance. On the clinical side, tight controls such as medication-administration processes, surgical procedures and infection control are in place to minimize errors and harm. Are you starting to feel like Alice chasing that rabbit down a hole?

The matrix

A common alternative to traditional top-down reporting is the matrix structure. A matrix structure is also a hierarchical, top-down reporting structure. The difference is that the reporting relationships are dual in nature (see image below). A manager or employee reports to two different people for two different functions, such as to a professional-practice leader and an operations manager, or to a functional manager and a product-line manager. A professional-practice leader provides direction and support related to professional performance standards, scope of practice and profession-specific regulatory expectations; the operations manager provides direction for the day-to-day work. Likewise, the functional manager prioritizes and reviews the daily work, while the product-line manager sets direction on product or service offerings.

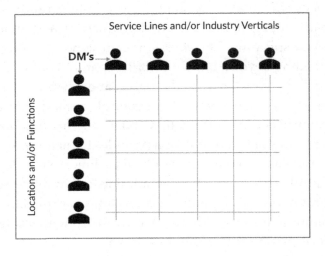

Matrix Organizational Structure

The matrix structure has some advantages. Resources can be used efficiently, since experts can be shared across projects. Products and projects are formally coordinated across functional departments. There is cross-pollination of information, which can speed up the decision-making process. And people are generally able to work more independently.

Matrix structures can have disadvantages as well, though. The skills required by managers and employees in a matrix model are different from those needed in traditional models. The most common problems we see are unclear manager accountabilities (sometimes intentional and sometimes not) and unhealthy competition between managers. Both situations create chaos and confusion. It's critical for dual managers to work from the same plan, be clear about accountabilities (no accountability vacations in this structure) and create a climate of psychological safety for their employees. This occurs through mutual goal-setting and creating clarity around values and expectations, first between the dual leaders and then with the employee. The skills and mindset of influence and negotiation replace leadership approaches of "power over" and managing through directives. Follow-up processes such as routine scheduled updates are critical to stay on track—manager to manager and manager to employee. The employee with dual managers also needs to develop new skills—skills that will help them communicate and navigate through competing priorities, personalities and expectations. When any of these skills are lacking, the matrix breaks down and frustration and distrust result.

Distributed and loose

In today's dynamic organizations, more is required than formal, top-down management reporting relationships. When greater specialization and expertise are needed, horizontal structures will leverage the information, knowledge and experience of all members. In horizontal structures, leadership is distributed to all levels of the organization—up, down and across (see image below). Decisions are made and solutions are developed by the person or team with expertise in the relevant area. Likewise, when tasks are highly interdependent and time is compressed, decisions are delegated to the people who understand the problem and the context. Events migrate up when they have unique circumstances or political implications that require an understanding of organizational nuances (Weick & Sutcliffe 2001).

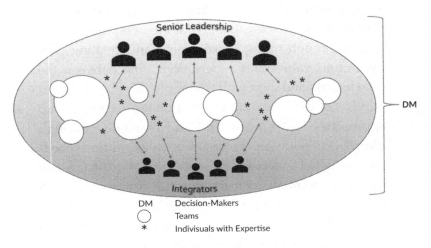

Distributed Leader Organizational Structure with
Integration Function

Such structures bring diverse people together formally and informally, and these people create value through their contributions. This value is a business asset that's critical for higher-quality decision-making and problem-solving. An example of a horizontal structure is a team within a team—performance-improvement teams (teams that continue in their current role and spend up to 20% of their time on special projects), squads (innovative teams that leave their day job for a specific period of time to work on a potential new product or service), huddles (short-standing team meetings for just-in-time information and/or problem-solving), briefings (interactions used to attain clear, timely and effective communication), professional-practice groups, shared-governance councils, learning networks and self-forming groups. These groups form and dissolve as needed. They explore common problems or opportunities and bring their expertise to the table to create new knowledge and develop innovative solutions. Where do we sign up?

While certain tight controls are still needed, as discussed, there's a movement to more loose controls that interject corporate-level perspectives into the team or group processes and promote the flow of information and knowledge across the organization. This is accomplished through simple rules or guidelines related to self-organization, empowerment and internal communication. Such loose controls include executive-level sponsorship of teams, the development of team charters with clear deliverables and timelines, timed progress reports and non-hierarchical communication guidelines and capabilities.

While horizontal structures provide more autonomy and allow for an exchange of ideas, they do come at a cost, including meeting and training time, as well as the cost of retraining managers as they shift their authority to others. While there may be a loss of efficiency in the short term due to training, structural support and coaching time, the expectation is that there will be a significant benefit to the organization in turbulent times that results in greater innovation and effectiveness.

Coordination and integration

As organizations grow and become more complex, horizontal structures can become unwieldly. They need a more formalized coordination and integration function. Resilient organizations always consider both the organization's long-term strategic needs and its day-to-day operations. Both views are critical to the organization's sustainability. In dynamic organizations with horizontal structures (multiple teams and networks working, solving problems and making decisions across multiple sites), it's critical to have mechanisms in place that enable an understanding of the system's environment and performance. Through structures that monitor the system's dynamics, new knowledge can be obtained, translated, communicated and acted on to enhance the organization's resilience. Expertise, accountabilities, capabilities and gaps can be identified and shared.

Organizational intelligence, coordination and integration are strengthened through insight into these five dynamics across the enterprise:

- Senior leadership direction—understanding and buy-in of the vision and goals to achieve the mission

- Operational systems—the effectiveness of the core products and services at the local level

- Business intelligence—access to needed data, information, knowledge and expertise

- Learning and innovations—communication of findings from real-time situations, such as critical events and rapid-cycle improvement processes

- Centralized functions—the impact of centralized functions (on the continuum of value to waste) at the business unit level

System integration and coordination work is a disciplined approach that requires focused accountabilities and technological support. Focused accountabilities occur through roles designed specifically for this function—such as a chief integration or sustainability officer, or a high-level transformation office. These positions are often supported by a small team of people across the organization. Integrators (not interrogators!) are leaders and team members with a broader view of the organization than a typical department or team leader. They have an enhanced view through timely data and information feeds, as well as through two-way access to the members, regardless of their location. This helps them see the opportunities to create value, such as by combining diverse skills and expertise across units and spotting "structural holes" that need to be filled (Ancona, Backman & Isaacs 2019).

The system integration and coordination team members work across boundaries and turfs, mindful of environment, commitment, expertise, problems and unexpected situations. The goal is to develop a more complete understanding of the organization—systems, emerging opportunities, risks and changes in the external environment—and act more effectively. Acting more effectively, in turn, frees up resources that can then focus on innovation, research and development and strategic goals.

Organizational Attributes and Structural Choices

Organizational Attributes	Top-Down (Command and control)	Distributed (Empowerment)	Matrix (Shared accountability)
Speed (to market, to decision-making, etc.)	3	1	2
Quality (of decision-making, products, etc.)	1	3	2
Communications (among internal stakeholders)	2	1	3
Engagement (commitment of all personnel)	1	3	2
Accountability (to values, goals and each other)	3	1	2
Risk management (avoiding unwanted outcomes)	1	3	2
Leadership development (promote from within)	1	2	3
Customer focus (net promoter score)	1	3	2
Innovation (creativity and empowerment)	1	3	2

Rating structures against the above attributes:

1 = Least effective

2 = Effective

3 = Most effective

Structural energy

Have you ever bought a house that wasn't quite what you wanted? Or perhaps your family grew and your house no longer met your needs. So you knocked a wall out here and added a room there. Over time, you made additional structural adjustments. And at some point, you realized you created a monster—or something that just didn't work for you. Everyday pressures create new conditions and needs for your family.

Organizations, too, face pressures that impact their performance. The environment shifts, technology becomes outdated, the organization grows, complexity increases and leadership changes. Over time, it's clear that the organization's current state isn't driving the needed results and that structural adjustments are necessary to mobilize the requisite energy and achieve excellence.

Though restructuring may be needed, it should not be taken lightly. It consumes time and resources and slows down efficiency in the short term. And many restructuring efforts fail completely. In the 1990s, for example, during the "reengineering management" craze, about two-thirds of reengineering efforts in Fortune 500 companies failed due to flawed thinking. Some of these efforts were even catastrophic, resulting in organizational collapse (Bolman & Deal 2013). We've been called in on many occasions to help leaders rescue an organization from a failed restructuring—a process designed by unenlightened leaders with no sound science to guide them. While we appreciate the work, the toll on the organization is tremendous.

✳
Poor design kills the magic
✳

There is no one ideal structure. The structure needs to change as the organizational situation changes (see table above). There are times for top-down leadership and times for a more collaborative and distributed leadership approach. The evidence shows us that in general, horizontal structures work best for complex and fast-paced organizations; hierarchical structures work best for troubled companies; and matrix structures work well for mature, stable organizations. That said, evidence-based principles are needed to guide organizations through the nuances of major and minor restructures to enhance and #ChannelTheEnergy.

The guiding principles for redesigning structures are listed below and described in more detail in the following sections.

- The structure is in synch with the culture

- The structure supports the workforce in its daily work

- The structure connects to the customer

- The structure supports the needs of leaders and workers for loose and tight control

- The structure promotes alignment of centralized functions with the system's strategic priorities

- The structure supports communication, collaboration, information flow and learning

In synch

Culture is the members' collective expectations and behaviors. When the structure isn't in synch with the current culture, or simply overlooked, an organization misdirects energy and resources. For example, in an action culture, it's important for members to have the knowledge and resources necessary to take the appropriate actions. The expectations are that information is shared quickly and openly with those who need it and that decisions are made at all levels of the organization. The structure, to be in synch, must support information-sharing, rapid communication, clear decision-making accountabilities and transparency around decisions and their outcomes. (Stop—check that heart rate and make sure you aren't breaking out in a cold sweat!) When the culture and structure are compatible, there's a greater understanding of expectations. When they're not, there's confusion, circular work, rework, cynicism and blame. This ultimately results in an episode of *Leaders Gone Wild* and has all the warning signs of science and reality colliding to create stupid!

Bumfuzzled

We often hear complaints from those in the trenches about how difficult it is to get their work done. New technologies are implemented without end-user input, resulting in workflows that bog people down. Equipment isn't available or in working condition.

There's a lack of information and direction that results in improvisation, guess work and rework at the point of service. And these structural problems create a bewildering quagmire of chaos for managers. (Forget Alcoholics Anonymous—how about Managers Anonymous!) Sadly, those at the top of the organization are often oblivious to these problems or, worse, blame the managers below them for the results of the structures. Sound familiar?

The end goal is to have structures that make it easier for the workforce to do the right things. This requires an understanding of the work. Yes, managers (of operations and functions) must understand the work their employees do. They can gain understanding through rounding, observation, data review and identifying patterns and trends. It involves asking questions and listening with an open mind. And it even means walking in your employees' shoes—just make sure you're not wearing their dirty socks!

The hip bone's connected to the leg bone

Organizational line-of-sight to the customers' ongoing wants and needs is a critical organizational competence—be they a client, consumer or patient. As our customers move away from a one-size-fits-all approach to services and products, so must we. Understanding the perspectives of the intended recipients of the products and services not only improves them, but also ignites the passion of the organizational members (Gulati 2019).

In organizations and industries with a heavy concentration of professionals who serve as agents to their customers, such as healthcare, law and financial investment, the customer-connection risks are even greater. An agent is someone who's authorized to act or decide on behalf of another (a principal) because the principal is incapable of choosing or executing the correct course of action as successfully as their designated agent (Hazard 1996). In other words, the principal customer is dependent on the agent expert, which makes them vulnerable. The physician-patient relationship is a great example of this. It's characterized by an asymmetry of knowledge and capabilities. This can create a significant disconnect and tendency to supplant the customer's perspectives and needs for the professionals.

Multiple structural supports enable customers to connect with organizational members. Examples include formalized processes that routinely involve the customer in the product or service design, technology and processes to obtain customers' feedback, customer participation on organizational committees and volunteer assignments by customers within the organization. And for organizations defined by agent-principal relationships, it's critical to have professional peer-review structures in place that include the customer's voice and perception.

Enough protection—but not too much

Because organizations need to be both adaptable and reliable in today's fast-paced world, special attention must be given to balancing these two attributes. Reliable operations require management of the system's inherent risks, but they can be overdone.

Barriers, redundancies and recoveries are essential controls meant to protect the workers and organization from error and harm. Barriers are guardrails to keep us out of trouble. Examples of barriers include laws, regulations, policies and job descriptions. Redundancies provide additional checks and balances (e.g., a two-person check before administration of a high-risk medication, second opinions before surgery, a signature requirement for invoice payment). Built-in recovery functions help correct when things go wrong. Recoveries include having a lifesaving medication, such as Narcan, available to reverse an overdose. Or having a spare tire in your trunk. Or having an extra set of clean clothes in your toddler's backpack.

*

Have the right guardrails

*

But when controls are overdone, they create unnecessary constraints, inefficiencies and costs and actually interject new risks. These risks come through work-arounds and/or the inability to adapt to changing conditions as needed due to structural straitjackets. For example, when locks are on doors that need to be accessed frequently, we often find the door propped open with a doorstop. When multiple layers of security are put in place to access information needed routinely by employees, shortcuts are created. It's critical to design processes that balance the workers' efficiency with the system's risks and make it easier to do the right thing.

No more running on autopilot

As organizations grow in size and complexity, they move toward centralized functions that support the business units (e.g., human resources, compliance, finance and information technology services). But these centralized functions also compete with the business units for resources and priorities. When their philosophy is to serve at the pleasure of the business units, they often find their resources are spread too thin. They quickly struggle with competing priorities and find they cannot be all to all. And when they put themselves first, above the business units, they might end up diverting resources to activities that make little difference to the organization's overall business objectives. They are perceived as serving themselves rather than their customers. Neither is optimal.

Centralized functional units or services best serve the overall organization when they're structured to closely align with the system's strategic priorities. Rather than compete with the business units, they provide value to them. For example, when an organizational strategy changes from hiring cheap labor to investing in talent, human resources ideally shifts their strategies and structures from hiring and onboarding entry-level positions quickly to identifying and hiring talent and investing in front-line retention.

A change in approach requires introspection, inquiries and dialogue, agreement with stakeholders on which capabilities and systems to invest in and, ultimately, communication of the strategies, priorities and rationale to the members. A helpful communication tool is a service agreement between the functional unit and its customers that outlines expectations and accountabilities. It's reviewed and agreed upon by both parties. As the system's strategies change, so does the service agreement.

Filling in the gaps

Information is critical to learning and adapting. Without information, people create their own story— leaders, members and customers alike. They obtain information through the Internet (if it's on the Internet, it must be true), at the coffee shop (an additional shot of caffeine accelerates "creative" thinking) or through anecdotal stories (reality is not critical for a sensational story!). Assumptions, rumors and gossip fill the void. Rather than focusing on problem-solving, people focus on filling information gaps. Time is wasted and people cannot do their best work.

*

Where, oh where, has our purpose gone?

*

Our old structures cannot accommodate today's fast pace and volume of information. Quarterly updates and staff meetings, monthly rounding and weekly newsletters aren't enough. Nor are biannual town halls and press releases. Structures are needed to promote a rapid flow of information vertically and horizontally—to the organizational members as well as to the customers. Technology is a great enabler of this flow but needs to be accompanied by other structural supports (e.g., routine leader/manager rounding, data analytics, decision-support systems, daily face-to-face huddles, electronic messaging boards, access to learning tools and customer-liaison roles).

These evidence-based guidelines for redesigning structure are instrumental when we change the way we channel the energy at the local and organizational levels to better serve our customers and honor and align our team members' talents and capabilities.

Keeping it real

CREATING THE CONDITIONS FOR SUCCESS

A colleague once worked for an organization that used a little blue symbol to line up their printed label with their logo. The organization even had a fifteen-minute one-on-one training session on the "proper" way to label things. Supervisors stood watch over those first 100 labels or so to make sure staff knew the proper procedure. Who knew there were so many rules as to the when, what, how and why of labeling! People (at all levels of the organization) agonized over the placement of these labels (alignment, location, etc.) and missed deadlines when the logo wasn't lined up to the exact specification and everything had to be scrapped and recreated.

The wasted time, energy and supplies added to cost overruns on projects. Watching these brilliant individuals lose their s*%t over a label was fascinating. Image is important, process is important, but I guarantee you this: most people never gave label alignment as a reason for not winning a proposal. *However*, because they were indeed late in delivering proposals due to this process and a fanatic quest for perfection, the awards were fewer. Were there other options? Yes—lighten up on "perfection control" (unless labeling is so high risk it can kill) or redesign the label process to make it easy to do the right thing. Either solution would have done.

ENGAGING THE TEAM

In years past, I worked with a committee tasked with eliminating costs across an entire system, not just a business unit. When I joined this discussion as the executive sponsor, I watched as "the rules of engagement" unfolded during a meeting. They were very specific and restrictive, only allowing for conversations about a person's area of direct responsibility. I looked around the room. Staff were looking at the clock or their phones, slumped in their chairs—they had absolutely no energy for yet another meeting that took up their time and yielded little results. Time to put the brakes on this approach.

In my opinion, the best ideas usually come from outside your close group. I requested that we lighten the guidelines a bit and have everyone come to the next meeting with three ideas that could help improve costs and/or performance anywhere in the organization. I encouraged them to look at things through a different lens—as if they were the customer. Most people interacted daily with staff from all areas of the business and at all levels. The perspective of other members could elicit a robust dialogue that might trigger some innovative thinking to help achieve the objectives.

At the next meeting, there was a healthy buzz in the room. People were already discussing their ideas before the meeting started. By the time everyone had gathered, the excitement was palpable. All were prepared to present their ideas and were eager for the discussion. Not one person had fewer than three ideas. There were some uncomfortable moments when certain ideas were discussed, but all were easily mitigated with a reminder that we were in this together—accountable to each other for an open and honest discourse. We owned the outcomes.

Subsequent meetings were just as engaging, and the team saw double-digit improvement in year one of the committee's overall improvement plan.

IMPROVING THE FLOW OF INFORMATION THROUGH HUDDLES

We worked with an organization that was struggling to move patients efficiently through the ED and meet their medical and emotional needs. The patients were backed up and leaving before even being seen. Quality and customer scores were in the toilet, and the ED physicians and staff seemed completely disinterested in doing anything differently.

A new, young star of a manager decided to take things into her own hands. She identified critical processes and related measures for the ED that would help them focus on all the right things. She enlisted the help of an analyst in another department to pull data together twice a day, rather than quarterly. She then collaborated with ED physician leadership to create the expectations and support for a team huddle every twelve hours within the department to review expectations, data and performance. The ten-minute huddles were to be attended by all staff and physicians on the shift for the purpose of reviewing the previous day's metrics and making adjustments to improve their performance during the current shift.

Suddenly, she had their attention. At first, they groaned and complained. Then they began brainstorming and problem-solving. They spontaneously formed small performance-improvement teams to focus on workflow changes. Eventually they started a friendly competition to see which team could outperform the other. Their performance started to climb. They began to have pride in their work and progress. Others noticed and gave them positive feedback, including senior leaders and board members. All because one young star decided she could make a difference. And she did!

⋆ Titter time: Channeling the energy ⋆

"I am currently experiencing life at the speed of fifteen WTFs per hour."
—Unknown

 Self-Help

Channel the energy. While senior leaders have the authority to change an organization's overall structures, managers can impact the structures in their area of influence as well. This exercise is to help you focus on one critical group as you redesign your playbook.

Reflect on your area of responsibility and consider these questions:

- Of your employee groups, which is most critical to delivering the results in your area of influence (e.g., nurses, accountants, IT specialists, salespeople, etc.)?

  _____

  _____

  _____

  _____

  _____

  _____

- What resources (e.g., equipment, information, time) do they need to do their work well daily?

  _____

  _____

  _____

  _____

  _____

  _____

- Do they have easy access to these resources? If not, what structural changes can you influence to make this happen (e.g., remove unnecessary controls, enhance data management, improve the equipment-repair process, and/or redesign workflows)?

_____

_____

_____

_____

_____

_____

- Identify ways you can enlist your team's expertise to make these structural changes in your area of influence.

_____

_____

_____

_____

_____

10

Performance Expectations: Be Careful What You Measure

Who doesn't love a good advertisement that has you believing if you only take that tiny pill, you too will soon be running down the beach in your skimpy bikini with the wind in your hair, a gorgeous tan and a model-buff body? Fast-forward a few weeks and little has changed except you have less money to spend, are bloated, and feel frustrated that pounds haven't fallen off and that what you see in the mirror is still nothing like that woman sprinting on the beach without breaking a sweat. Where did you go wrong? You forgot that in the fine print was the reality check: you have to change your daily menu to jump-start your system, monitor calorie intake and, most importantly, exercise daily. Geez—it was supposed to be so easy! Your brief journey into fantasyland was enjoyable until that digital scale went tilt. Fortunately, you're bought back to reality and realize that what you measure matters.

The L3 Fusion Model:
A journey to transformation

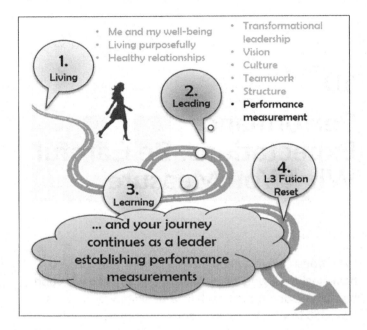

What we measure matters. (We'll avoid the obvious reference!) Success, or failure, is measured and communicated by metrics. They drive our behavior and are a powerful force for change. We don't need to look far to see how metrics have resulted in improvements and/or misconduct. Research shows that when it comes to change initiatives, having performance metrics in place is more important than the content of the intervention (Bennet & Bennet 2004). Metrics can mean the difference between success and failure. Performance measurement can also lead to bad behaviors, such as bribery and fraud, when targets are high and incentives are perceived as significant. For example, overly aggressive sales targets or referral pressures linked to financial, recognition or promotional incentives too often result in integrity lapses and illegal or unethical acts. In the case of Enron, it led to prison time. For companies such as Siemens, Volkswagen and Teva Pharmaceutical, it led to the destruction of shareholder value (Healy & Serafeim 2019). We need to be thoughtful about what we measure.

While measurement matters, just because we can measure something, doesn't mean we should. Too often we see organizations that are obsessed with the process of measurement at the cost of not improving the business. Some organizations have a bias toward improvement of efficiency (doing things at a lesser cost) at the expense of effectiveness (doing the right things). Other organizations simply have a bias toward busyness—collecting data, measuring activities and spending time in meetings that never really get to the hard work of improving anything.

Ubiquitous metrics

Performance measurements, when designed well, keep us on track. When designed poorly, they can take us down the wrong path and get us into trouble: #BeCarefulWhatYouMeasure.

Measurement transgressions always start small. They build and ultimately snowball because they become embedded in the base measures and our evaluators (boards, investors, regulators, etc.) expect to see them continuously improve. When measurements start going the wrong way, everyone jumps on the "not me—must be you" campaign. Whether you're measuring emission levels, college ratings, revenue recognition or realization of assets, the how is just as important as the what. That's why we have auditors (and other independent validators)—to make sure the how is done right.

Performance metrics come from a variety of places. External parties have high expectations and requirements for organizations and professionals that cannot be ignored without significant risk. As professionals, we're held to standards by our state or national regulators and/or certification bodies. A breach of ethics or professional practice can have dire consequences, such as loss of license. Likewise, most industries are highly regulated, and regulatory noncompliance can carry a high penalty financially, reputationally and personally (yes, jail time—and we don't look good in orange). Our performance also bears scrutiny from the public itself with electronically accessible quality scores, credit ratings and stock prices. And then there's the prolific customer-satisfaction feedback available on mandated websites and social media. (Ugh—how is your stress level right now? Hang in there. Take a few deep breaths and let's keep going.)

And if that isn't enough, we also have obligations and requirements that come from inside the organization as well. At the highest level, these comprise the strategic direction (vision), priorities and goals that drive the organization's time, energy and resources. They're typically tied to external requirements and/ or competitive forces that require efforts—for example, a financial turnaround, realignment or escalating improvement. This strategic direction is the why behind much of the work we do. The strategic goals are translated into broad "outcome measures" for the organization—measures that quantify large-scale characteristics such as overall productivity, revenue and quality. Contributors to these broad outcomes are many. The organization's structures, leadership decisions, processes, behaviors and culture all impact the

results/outcomes in one way or another. It's important, therefore, that these outcomes be further translated into specific actions and measures that will help
move the organization toward these outcomes at the
local level. Approach it as learning a new language
that opens the door to innovative ways of thinking to
influence others and/or outcomes.

Guidelines for measuring performance—I have a headache

Measurement drives performance—so it's critical
for leaders to have measures in place that communicate the right expectations and inform the activities and decisions in their areas of responsibility.
Evidence-based guidelines help us develop effective
performance-management systems and have these
characteristics:

- The organization's vision, strategy and strategic goals serve as the foundation

- Performance measures link the local activities or processes to the high-level organizational goals and outcomes

- Measures provide feedback as close to real time as possible

- Information is valid, reliable, meaningful and easy to use

- The measurement system enables benchmarking and progress monitoring

Each of these are described in more detail in the following sections.

Vision, strategy and strategic goals are the foundation

Because the organization's vision and strategy ideally drive the organization's time, energy and resources, it's important to know what they are and why they exist at this time in the organization's life cycle. This often requires a deeper understanding of the organization's history and the underlying beliefs and assumptions that support the strategies and goals. This knowledge helps us translate the strategic priorities into needed actions in our areas of accountability. It helps us connect the what to the why. If you don't know, ask your one-up supervisor. Make it a point to be informed. It's difficult leading people to the promised land when we don't know where it is or why we're going there.

Begin with the end in mind

Start by measuring for the future. Consider what success looks like, how it will be measured and how you'll know when you've gotten there. Then measure where you are today. By developing specific measures for their teams, leaders tailor the activities that are important to achieving the organizational goals and connect the work of their people to these goals. For example, in a health system (organizational level) losing significant market share, the CEO called out a strategic goal of improving their customers' perceptions of their service. At the local level, a unit manager determined she'd focus her team on treating patients with courtesy and respect and created two strategies to support this goal—answering call lights within a prescribed period of time and creating scripted questions that demonstrated respect for patients' concerns. She connected the dots from the local goals and measures to the strategic ones. The nursing staff understood what was being measured, how it was being measured and why it was being measured. This led to confidence in the information and a deeper understanding of how their choices and actions in the unit impacted the patients' overall perception of their hospital care.

A day late and a dollar short

There's nothing like receiving critical feedback a day late. Remember the movie *Runaway Bride*? If only she'd learned some important facts about herself before the first engagement that led to her flight down the aisle. Of course, the movie wouldn't have been nearly as much fun, but you get the point. While delays exist in most feedback processes, advances in technologies are making more and more real-time data available. We're evolving from looking at history to forecasting the future and looking at the present to inform our current actions. The more real time the data, the better we understand how our actions affect the outcomes we're measuring and the sooner we can modify our behaviors and activities.

Smart leaders take the time to figure out their data needs. This can be overwhelming to do on our own (and that's okay), so find a partner—a person who lives and breathes data, such as a business analyst—and work with them. A business analyst helps translate data needs into "technology speak" so that the data analyst on the other end can provide us with the needed information. Our skill as leaders is to be able to translate this data into meaningful information that helps meet our business needs.

Unpack it, explain it, repeat it

A valid measure is one that accurately measures what's supposed to be measured. For example, a pedometer measures the number of steps a person takes and estimates distance. It's valid for step accuracy but not for accurately tracking distance—individuals who have short legs may take twice as many steps as their long-legged friends. The good news is that while they go the same distance, short people get a better workout. (This may be an invalid statement but it's what we tell ourselves.)

Reliability is about the stability of a measure or test from one use to the next. A cardiac monitor is reliable when it consistently measures the patient's heart rate accurately. Information that's valid and reliable is trustworthy. It can be unpacked, explained, repeated.

How many times have you tried to do a deep dive on data and found that the underlying assumptions were different, the data was coming from different sources at different times and measured in different ways and when questioned, the analyst exclaimed, "I'm not sure how we came up with that." This is not a recipe for success. Here are some practices to adopt to make sure the information that you end up with is valid, reliable and meaningful.

- **Get clear**—Start by getting clear about the question you want to answer, or the problem you're trying to solve. Boil it down to its essence. Remove the noise. Getting to this type of clarity is often an iterative process. Work with a business analyst who understands the data sources and methodologies. This will help you avoid the swirl that can be caused by multiple functions, leaders and staff going after the same data for different reasons, or the swirl that occurs from getting the wrong data. By asking a series of questions, both parties can think through what data is needed (input) to get the right information (output) to better understand the problem and/or inform the needed action. This process saves time on the back end through the avoidance of multiple reworks.

- **Understand the data**—When you receive the report (output), make sure that you understand the data, including its source and timeframe. The analyst should define what each data point represents and provide meaningful information to end users about the data set's context.

- **Perform quality checks**—A quality check ensures the data is valid. A common mishap in data analysis is unclear data timelines. For example, when looking at a new budget report for your department, it's important to know if the information is based on the current fiscal year with forecasted projections through the end of the year or if it's simply year-to-date.

- **Present data with meaning**—Present data in ways that promote rapid understanding and are meaningful to the end users. Know your audience. Our team members have a variety of educational backgrounds and experiences. They all bring something of value to the table, but when we present information in ways that they don't understand, we devalue their contributions. They often feel disrespected. Leaders use a variety of approaches when presenting information to their teams, including visualization techniques (graphs, flow charts, pictures, colors), descriptors and discussions about the implications and underlying assumptions. But let's avoid those hundred-plus-page reports that could substitute as a doorstop!

- **Promote information accessibility**—Make information accessible to those who need it. Don't be a data hoarder! This is achieved through a variety of approaches, including sharing with performance-improvement teams, in staff meetings and through educational sessions; posting in appropriate areas; and/or providing through data portals and embedding in decision-support tools.

Gauging your team's performance

Benchmarking is the process of identifying, understanding and adapting best practices from others to help an organization improve its performance. It's an activity that looks outward to find high performance and then measure actual business operations against these performance goals to obtain competitive advantages.

A pragmatic approach to benchmarking for organizational success is to first find meaningful measurements to gauge your team's performance. There are industry standards for many of these benchmarks and comparative databases with details about the nuances. Some of these standards are proprietary but many are available through professional and trade organizations. Many are published. Know where you and your team stand. Look for best practices to improve your team's effectiveness. Measure the improvements. Document and share the progress with the team and key stakeholders. This isn't an exercise in looking better—it's an exercise in being better!

A balanced approach to performance measurement

Many organizations use the balanced scorecard approach at the corporate level to obtain performance measurement guidance and feedback. It's based on the research of Harvard Business School professor Robert Kaplan and his colleague David Norton (1996, 2001) and exists in a variety of forms. The strength of this approach is that it's not focused purely on financial measures—it's more holistic. In an era of complexity, a balanced approach to performance measurement is needed to create and show value. We outline five perspectives, or views of the organization, as the starter set for every leader. The first four perspectives are from Kaplan and Norton's original set—financial, internal business, customer, and innovation and learning. The fifth perspective is a common add and one we recommend for organizations that are heavily dependent on human capital—the human experience. Each perspective begins with the primary question that needs to be answered, followed by additional questions to help focus us on the right priorities at the current time. As times change, so must the answers. We've adapted the questions for each of the five perspectives to be relevant to any leader, regardless of their level of authority in the organization. Please note that the questions put the accountability on the leader. We don't assume that the leader is doing this work independently, though. Rather, we make the point that it's through the leader's leadership that teams and key stakeholders are aligned and effective. The five perspectives and key questions for a balanced scorecard follow.

1. Financial perspective—Answer the question *"How do I look to my supervisor?"*
   What (not how) am I contributing to the organization's financial performance? Do I understand my costs and are they at an effective and efficient level? Do I have a plan to deliver high performance at a reasonable cost? Do I understand the risks in achieving my plan? Do I have a way to manage the risks? Do I understand the regulatory requirements that impact my area and am I in compliance? How do I know this?

2. Internal business perspective—Answer the question *"At what must I excel?"*
   Am I focused on critical internal operations that are important to the overall organization? How am I meeting the needs and demands of my internal customers (other departments, leaders, professional groups) as they relate to satisfaction, quality, regulatory issues, safety, productivity,

cycle time and / or employee competence? How do I know this?

3. Customer perspective—Answer the question *"How do my customers (consumers, clients, patients, investors) view my leadership?"*
What do our external customers expect and need? What's important to them and am I giving it to them? How am I delivering on their expectations as they relate to time, efficiency of services, quality, safety, cost and performance? How do I know this?

4. Innovation and learning perspective—Answer the question *"How can I continue to improve and create value for the organization?"*
What new products or services have I developed? What improvements have I made in current service or product offerings? What outside knowledge have I brought into the organization and shared with others? What lessons from failure have I shared?

5. Human experience perspective—Answer the question *"How do my employees (including contractors) and key stakeholders see me?"*
What do my employees, contractors and key stakeholders expect and need from me? What's important to them and am I giving it to them? Am I attracting and retaining talent? How do I know this?

Measure your value

Once you've considered the five perspectives, think through the actions needed for success in the current environment. Seek out the wisdom of team members, colleagues and supervisors. Their perceptions and input are invaluable and will help inform the rest of the process. Then it's time to develop measurable goals for the identified actions for each of the five perspectives, creating your own balanced scorecard. This process serves as a guide.

- **Goal**—For each perspective, ask what problem you're trying to solve and what exactly you want to accomplish. Make sure it's important to the organization. Think about not just present but also future needs. Be specific. Be bold. You have a unique understanding, so use this goal-setting process as an opportunity to create awareness.

- **Measurement**—Determine how you'll know when you've reached this goal. Whenever possible, quantify your response with a numeric value. Consider what data and metrics are available to you, how you'll determine current performance and how you'll measure progress along the way. Develop a reachable target measure that's valid, reliable, meaningful and accessible.

- **Timeline**—Determine when you'll achieve this goal.

- **Resources**—Determine if you have the resources needed to achieve this goal in the above timeline. If not, determine how you'll get the resources and/or adjust the timeline as needed to use existing resources.

- **Documentation**—Write the goals using measurable language. For example, "Department A will decrease their employee-turnover rate from 24% to 18% over the next twelve months."

- **Follow-up**—Share the goals with those who will make them happen. Determine the key actions (initiatives) that will help you achieve them. Develop a plan and process to get there with the resources and timeline identified. Think of ways to involve your team and others to gain insights, build enthusiasm and get buy-in. Consider researching best practices, developing rewards for successes along the way, developing tools and training, and promoting learning.

Always be prepared to show the value that you and your team bring to the table. You are the best advocate for you and your people! As formal and informal leaders in organizations, we continuously influence the way the work gets done. Take the time to measure and quantify the positive changes you impact over time as well as the lessons learned during failed attempts. Document these. When we routinely share these contributions, we show the value we bring to the table. Celebrate progress and lessons learned with the team.

Keeping it real

MISSING THE FOREST FOR THE TREES

How often have you heard the legendary statement "I'm doing okay against budget"? Many managers are excited when they can express this, and look to others for applause. Reality check—the organization is losing money and is in violation of its lender requirements. So your performance compared to budget doesn't matter if you continue to lose money.

Organizations spend months developing a budget, making changes, presenting to management and then making more changes. There's an urgency to get it perfect, even down to the penny! But when it's time to roll out the budget, it's clear that in the first month, most units missed their target. Surprise! They spent so much time in the weeds they forgot to ensure that all the variables that could impact the budget were included.

It's decided a balanced scorecard will be developed, and before you know it, there's a document that's five pages long and trying to measure everything. First, this is impossible. Second, it takes up too much time and resources. And third, most of the measures don't impact performance/outcomes, so you're back to an organization that loses money.

This is leadership failing to recognize what matters. In broad categories, the most important measures are those that impact customer satisfaction, financial performance and product or service quality. And even when measures show a problem, it often takes a cultural reset to address it. Whether you're working with a profit and loss statement, a balance sheet or a balanced scorecard, if the numbers don't measure up to independent outside benchmarks, you're budgeting for mediocrity. And, my friends, entrenched mediocrity kills organizations!

BE CAREFUL WHAT YOU MEASURE

A prominent health system was focusing on improving the wait times for cardiac patients in their emergency room (ER). The focus was on getting them out of the ER quickly and into the cath lab so that lifesaving procedures could be done. They had a goal of improving time from ER to cath lab by 30% and were comparing their performance to national benchmarks. Administration was monitoring this number closely. As a result, the dedicated ER staff quickly moved patients from a safe setting in the ER (where physicians and other team members were present) to the cath lab upstairs, where they waited alone with their unstable patient until the on-call cardiologist and cath lab staff arrived. The ER nurses didn't have the support they needed to safely care for these patients.

As the organization celebrated the reduction in ER wait times, patients were experiencing adverse events such as delays in treatment of chest pain and blood pressure support. None of this was deliberate (stupid, perhaps, not well thought out, perhaps, but not deliberate). It was unforeseen and unrecognized by the decision-makers. The measures set up incentives that drove behaviors that had negative consequences for patients. They were making some processes more efficient at the expense of effectiveness. Be careful what you measure.

⋆ Titter time: Measurement ⋆

"The best measure of a woman's honesty
isn't her tax return. It's the zero adjust on her
bathroom scale."
—Adapted from Arthur C. Clarke

 Self-Help

Create your own balanced scorecard.

Start with one perspective and, using the score-card template shown, go through the process described in this chapter. If your organization has a strategic balanced scorecard, connect your goals to the strategic goals. Then keep going until you have at least one initiative for each of the five perspectives.

The Leader's Balanced Scorecard

Organizational and/or Leader Vision: _____

_____

_____

_____

Perspective	Goal	Measure	Key actions / initiatives	Target Date
Finance				
Internal business				
Customer				
Innovation-learning				
Human experience				

11

Ignorance Is Never Bliss: We Must Be Continuously Learning To Be Successful

Remember playing Telephone? Given the phrase "Donna swept the dank dark space," you eagerly start the game. Down the line your friends whisper the phrase that's beginning to garner giggles and snickers. Finally, everyone bursts out laughing when the last person announces: "Do you sweat when you drink?" Others clearly didn't hear the same thing as you did! Misinterpretation can result in humor but also confusion that can be detrimental to an organization.

The L3 Fusion Model:
A journey to transformation

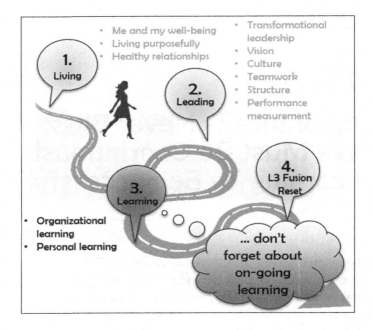

How many times have you sat in a meeting with someone and come away with a significantly different view of the information shared in it than they did? This distortion occurs because our individual tendencies impact what we notice and hear and how we interpret what we notice and hear. In other words, our uniqueness impacts our learning.

Learning is much more than passive receipt of information. It's the act of interpreting our own experience—our direct and indirect experiences. This interpretation is unique to each of us and is enabled or constrained by our past experiences and how we make sense of the world.

It's difficult to know if we're interpreting the world correctly or accurately because there's data and information that we don't see or sense. Successful individuals are those who reflect on their own thinking and experiences, who learn as they go and who approach problems in a variety of ways. They're able to make meaning out of the experience they and others have in the world. When people function without introspection and reflection, they don't understand either their environments or themselves but feel as though they do (Weick & Sutcliffe 2001).

Fundamental to personal and professional success is a commitment to lifelong learning: #OwnYourOwn-Learning.

This commitment requires an honest look at how we interpret our experiences and make meaning out of them. Through honest scrutiny of our thinking and expectations, or the practice of mindfulness, we can significantly improve our learning. This mindfulness begins with a better understanding and awareness of our human tendencies. Armed with this understanding, we can then create practices that counteract our negative tendencies and strengthen our positive ones.

> **If you think education is expensive, try ignorance.**
> —Derek Bock

Healthy learning practices include taking time to center ourselves—minimizing distractions promotes greater awareness of our present state. This practice is helpful particularly when we're feeling emotional. Other practices include staying open to diverse points of view (through active listening, promoting a curious spirit and being willing to change one's mind) and giving ourselves permission (full freedom!) to examine the validity of our beliefs—we can question them, reaffirm them, update them and even replace them. Ultimately, these mindfulness activities change the way we interpret our experiences, resulting in new learning.

How we think and learn

Learning often occurs when we notice something different. We must hold the difference in our mind long enough to make sense of it (for some of us, that could be quite a long time). When we become aware of the dissonance between what we think and the new information, we become more able to change our thinking (Dixon 1999).

Our learning is impacted by two distinct modes our mind uses to process information. The first is the attentional mode, which is limited, sequential, slow and effortful (e.g., memorizing a difficult formula or new and detailed information). Think of our attentional mode as a straw that can hold only seven peas. When you add an eighth pea, one falls out the other end. In attentional mode, we can retain only so much information and interruptions, noise and protruding thoughts take our attention away from the task at hand.

In automatic mode, we process familiar information rapidly and without conscious effort (e.g., identifying a medication by the look of its label; when asked to describe the label, the information is not within our consciousness). This processing mode lies beyond the direct reach of awareness, but its products (i.e., our words, images, feelings and actions) are available to our consciousness. In this mode, we go beyond processing the given information and supply missing data (accurate or not) through sensory or recalled information.

It would be a different world if only the attentional mode existed. We would have to work hard at remembering every little thing. Even small distractions could be significantly hazardous to our well-being and success. But the price humans pay for our ability to largely process information automatically is that perceptions, memories, thoughts and actions tend to err in the direction of the familiar and the expected. In other words, our mind makes things up without our being conscious of it.

Much of our learning occurs through our automatic mode over time and without our conscious awareness. Think about your ideas and feelings about love, politics, freedom, justice, beauty (some of us look in the mirror and still see ourselves as twenty-five, not fifty-five and beyond!). Each of these is impacted by exposure to the culture in which we live, as well as our own experiences. In fact, we alter these ideas and feelings over time as we retrieve our long-term memories. We reconstruct our remembrances, often automatically, and these reconstructions are often inaccurate, even though we think they're accurate (Dixon 1999).

Our habits of thought

Researchers in the field of cognitive psychology have studied the nature of human thinking and its impact on planning, decision-making and evaluation processes when dealing with complex problems (Dörner 1996; Weick & Sutcliffe 2001). We're often unaware of our human tendencies and how they impact our everyday learning. These five common habits of thought negatively impact learning, particularly in dynamic situations:

1. Insufficient consideration of processes in time

2. Focus on symptoms rather than the fundamental problem

3. Simplifying and economizing

4. Confirmation bias

5. Preserving an optimistic view of oneself

Insufficient consideration of processes in time creates problems in terms of delays and time pressure. When there's a delay between the time of one's action and the consequences of one's action, the consequences are poorly understood. For example, a senior manager's decision to change suppliers can have a negative impact at the point of service (e.g., inferior supplies or a decrease in productivity from lack of training) if this manager doesn't understand the connection.

At the other end of the spectrum, under time pressure, we tend to overdose on established measures (e.g., turning the thermostat up too high when one is cold, resulting in the room temperature becoming too hot).

The tendency to **focus on symptoms rather than the fundamental problem** means that all effort goes toward treating the symptoms and not toward solving the underlying problem because gaining an understanding of this problem is difficult and time consuming. We focus on the wrong problems and goals, neglecting the fundamental issue and its long-term considerations and consequences.

When we **simplify and economize**, we don't take side effects and long-term repercussions into account. Truth is commonly identified with comprehensibility and simplicity, and there's a lack of understanding of the system's complexity. Attributing a failure of an intervention or change to a single cause is often a simplification that misses the mark—e.g., explaining an unfavorable variance as just a bad budget instead of seeking to understand the underlying cause, or blaming a nurse for a medication error rather than looking at the multiple system contributors to that error.

Confirmation bias is the tendency to look for evidence that supports or confirms our own view. We act out of this tendency when we surround ourselves with people who think like us or tell us only what we want to hear. And we know that the higher up we are in an organization, the more filtered the information we receive is. This is a direct path to leadership failure. Another example of confirmation bias is crediting only the data that supports our project and discrediting the data that doesn't without further exploration.

Preserving an optimistic view of oneself is the tendency to exaggerate our abilities and accomplishments. This tendency is often seen in executives and is a delusional optimism. We all know people who suffer from this! Research into human cognition has traced this optimism to many sources, with one of the most powerful being the tendency of individuals to exaggerate their own talents, to believe they're above average. This tendency often lies outside the realm of our consciousness and reshapes the direction and course of our thought processes, leading to the "I may not always be right, but I am never wrong" syndrome. Our thinking shuts down precisely when we need it most.

> If I continue to believe as I have always believed,
> I will continue to act as I have always acted.
> If I continue to act as I have always acted,
> I will continue to get what I have always gotten.
> —Marilyn Ferguson

I can't hear you

Feedback can be an important aspect of learning. Feedback, as defined here, is the act of giving other people evaluative or corrective information about their performance. We can almost see new managers inflate when they're given this responsibility. They can't wait to tell people what they think of them. (Whoa! Let's put the brakes on.) The desired outcome is to strengthen, not harm, people and their performance. It's important to have a good understanding of the art and science behind effective feedback if we want it to result in learning.

When we hear the words "I want to give you some feedback," most of us go into fight-or-flight mode. Our brain perceives a threat (e.g., comments about our shortcomings) and triggers our sympathetic nervous system. This release of adrenaline narrows our focus and produces an adaptive response to the stressor. This response is appropriate for an immediate threat to life or limb but gets in the way of our thinking in other situations. It inhibits our thought processes as it narrows our breadth of attention and results in compromised thinking (and overactive sweat glands). Negative feedback, therefore, can lead to deflation, confusion, and impaired learning.

"Learning is less a function of adding something that isn't there than it is of recognizing, reinforcing and refining what already is" (Buckingham & Goodall

2019, p. 97). According to brain science, every time we learn, we forge a new neural pathway in our brain. And the neurons in our brain grow the most where they are already the most developed. When we provide feedback that focuses on shortcomings, the person goes into "shut-down mode" (I can't hear you!), muting access to existing neural circuits and impairing their emotions and perceptions. When we focus our feedback on what's working well, the recipient's parasympathetic system lights up, stimulating more neuron growth and sending them into "opened-up mode" (tell me more!) with a sense of well-being.

We commonly give two types of feedback—objective and subjective. The first type is given when the actions or knowledge necessary to minimally perform a job or task can be objectively defined in advance. The needed steps are often clearly defined in a procedure, protocol, rule or algorithm. If an individual performs a technical procedure incorrectly or cannot apply the needed knowledge to do the work, specific feedback can be helpful and useful. For example, checklists in airplane cockpits and operating rooms allow a third party to identify a deviation from the standard. Similarly, cooking recipes and clinical protocols have objective steps to follow and can be objectively evaluated.

The second type of feedback is much more subjective and self-centered. Subjective feedback is when an individual shares their opinion with another on how they can improve their performance (because, of course, they believe they know best). It assumes that the person providing the feedback has the insight and expertise and the other person does not. It also assumes that "my way should be your way." Both assumptions are overreaching, yet this process routinely occurs in organizations through formal and informal feedback mechanisms. This approach doesn't help others learn or improve their performance (Buckingham & Goodall 2019).

So how should we provide feedback in situations that go beyond objective definition to more abstract qualities? First, we need to believe that our evaluations are deeply colored by our own tendencies, biases and understanding of a situation. These biases, as outlined above, lead to more distortion than truth because they're beyond our awareness. And no amount of additional data eliminates this inherent bias. If you ask a group of artists to describe a beautiful woman, you'll get a whole host of responses because of the subjective nature of the request. And the same thing will happen when you ask people in a workplace to define its abstract qualities.

Second, we need to understand and believe that when it comes to subjective feedback, all we can do is share our own feelings, experiences, thoughts and reactions. When we phrase this feedback in words that reflect back on ourselves—words such as "I felt," "I experienced," "I believed"—we are speaking our truth and letting someone know where they stand with us.

While our words are important, so is our body language and our tone. Through a combination of our words, non-verbal body language and tone, we can offer feedback that is more empathetic, humble and accurate and that allows for more—more options, other opinions, additional exploration, new learning, etc. Finding the right combination requires preparation and intent.

*

Note to self: Keep learning!

*

Learning and performance are also enhanced when feedback focuses on strengths. When we receive feedback on what we're doing well, our neural pathways open up and are able to focus on the nuances of the situation, expanding our learning. We saw an example of this approach in a large academic hospital. A new, tentative young nurse saw a woman sobbing in the hallway outside a patient's room. The nurse stopped, put her hand on the woman's shoulder and quietly spoke to her. The manager watched this interaction from afar. When it was over, the manager approached the young nurse and said, "I noticed how you stopped to talk to that upset woman, gently put your hand on her shoulder and calmed her down. I'm not sure what you said to her, but I was impressed! I want you to think about your interaction with her, what you said and did, how you said and did it, and do more of that." Wow! The nurse did think about this conversation many times throughout the week. She considered what she did well and what she could have done even better. She described this as a great learning experience that gave her more confidence for the next uncomfortable interaction.

Feedback is personal. And excellence for each of us is a unique expression of who we are. Ask yourself, "What do I do best? How do I do it? What do I have a passion for?" When we focus only on our failures, we have difficulty visualizing success and understanding our patterns of excellence. We all benefit from looking at the outcomes of our actions. Resist the urge to focus on the negatives. When the outcomes are positive, take the time to deconstruct how you got there and to learn to be more excellent.

Organizational learning

Barriers

A paradox of organizational learning is that organizations can learn only through their individual members, but organizations often make it difficult for individual members to learn (Dixon 1999). Leaders sometimes knowingly and often unknowingly construct barriers that inhibit organizational learning. These learning barriers include:

- Information hoarding because of the belief that information is power (time for an intervention!)

- A heavy focus on short-term efficiency to the detriment of allowing time for organizational members to do it themselves (the "just give it to me and I'll do it all and tell you about it later" syndrome)

- Controls that are too tight, resulting in the member's inability to act on their learning (no one goes to school for micromanagement, but many sure excel at it)

- A culture that responds to a challenge to the data and/or the status quo with "we've always done it this way" (before you know it, thirty years have passed and the organization is still gathering dust)

- A pattern of asking for more and more data but never solving the problem ("If we just keep asking for data, they'll at least think we're doing something")

By intentionally designing personal and professional learning systems, we can replace negative behaviors with positive ones.

Enablers

Because learning is critical to the organization's ability to adapt and sustain itself, it's important to have internal and external learning strategies in place. Internal learning strategies for leaders at all levels of the organization include (Scott & Pringle 2018):

- Using learning systems that drive quality and performance, such as evidence-based learning tools and techniques, decision-support tools, data management systems, distributed online learning tools, action-learning programs, case studies and web-based discussions around real-life problems.

- Promoting learning methodologies that support systems thinking. These methodologies help us understand and anticipate the impact of local changes on the overall organization and vice versa. Six Sigma, Lean and Plan-Do-Study-Act are examples of these learning systems. Develop your personal toolkit.

- Developing adaptive space to connect, learn and solve problems. This occurs when we create structures that enable connection, share expertise and experience across boundaries, and develop new knowledge for innovation.

Learning strategies that promote external learning are also beneficial and include:

- Participating in external learning groups and programs, such as communities of interest and professional and trade organizations, as well as national certification programs and targeted education that fills an organizational gap.

- Connecting to outside expertise for consultation and advice. When expertise is needed to fill an internal knowledge or skill gap, consultants can be quite valuable, particularly when they impart their skill and knowledge to organizational members over time.

When we're willing and able to remove the barriers to learning and strengthen the learning enablers, we not only build an intelligent and productive workforce but also increase our ability to retain our workforce.

Own your own learning—regardless

While it's important for leaders to promote learning within the organization, the bottom line is that each of us needs to own our own learning—regardless.

Transformation is messy work in both our personal and organizational lives. It requires changing the way we think through a willingness to be curious, ask more questions, investigate the status quo, become more vulnerable and make mistakes, learn from them, adapt and move on. It's a personal investment that's our personal responsibility. It's an investment in both the short term and the long run.

There are many ways we can own our own learning, depending on our individual interests and needs. Below are a few to consider.

- Master a new skill or area of knowledge, one that will help you improve your performance. This may occur through informal learning and/or through workshops, webinars, certification processes and more formal education.

- Participate in a leadership learning network made up of diverse leaders from multiple professions, industries and even countries. These networks can expose us to diverse points of view and experiences that help us expand our thinking and approach our work in more innovative ways.

- Join a community of interest (a group that has a common passion or vision) and/or a community of practice (a professional group that shares a common set of expectations and accountabilities) to learn and network with others outside your organization.

- Find a mentor or mentor someone else. Mentorship is when a more experienced person takes an interest in the development of a less experienced person in whose shoes they once walked. They invest in the less experienced person by sharing the wisdom they've gained while traveling a similar path.

- Find a coach. This is a supportive and non-judgmental professional who will focus on your self-identified agenda, helping you diagnose and mitigate your blind spots, identify and leverage your unique strengths, create influence, manage conflict and accountability, clarify your goals and build better teams.

- Reach out to us. Your authors welcome the opportunity to assist you.

There are so many learning opportunities. It's important for each of us to find an approach that keeps us learning and growing in every season of our life.

 ## Keeping it real

RECEIVING FEEDBACK

Don't you love those performance reviews where you're asked to complete your own and then the evaluator chooses not to consider your comments? Clearly, they're totally committed to helping you learn and grow as a leader and provide constructive feedback! We all know reviews can be painful, but given the opportunity to participate in the process, both reviewer and reviewee should embrace it.

Cautionary tale—don't get lazy when it comes to the review process. Recently, someone was asked to complete her own review and submit it to her one-up. Having already had numerous issues with this one-up (e.g., not providing input on her performance, openly berating her for failures, taking credit for her work, etc.), she was ready to put the reviewer to a test. She completed the form with many falsehoods and ridiculous language and submitted it to her one-up. As "stupid" would have it, the reviewer cut and pasted the content without even a glance at it and submitted the form to HR with a note that it would be discussed with the manager by week's end. As you might imagine, HR read the evaluation and was stunned. While much of it was certainly chuckle worthy, most of it wasn't appropriate and HR knew that something was amiss. I'm sure you know how this situation ends—badly for all parties. How unfortunate that both reviewer and reviewee felt the need to impact this process in a negative manner. Be careful what you wish for—you just might get it!

ANOTHER FEEDBACK STORY

Have you ever walked into a room prepared to discuss your contribution to the organization for your performance review and instead your evaluator ends up talking about themselves? Next thing you know, an hour has gone by and you've learned about someone else's stellar career (not!) and how brilliant they are at managing situations (a true legend). Funny thing—you haven't learned one thing about your performance or what you could be doing better. Well, maybe you just did: never focus on yourself when giving someone feedback on their performance.

BENGAY MOMENTS

Do you ever live or lead by rote, missing many of the nuances around you—body language, minor changes in messaging, important seating arrangements, etc.? When we're preoccupied, distracted or running on autopilot, it's easy to make judgments or decisions based on what we expect to happen versus what's actually happening. It's easy to miss the boat.

Here's a personal example of this. One evening while camping with friends, I excused myself during a card game to use the restroom in their motor home. While there, I decided it would also be a good idea to brush my teeth. I picked up the tube on the side of the sink, vigorously brushed my teeth and went back to the card game. When I sat down, I said, "Wow, that is some hot toothpaste!" About half an hour later, my friend visited the restroom. He called out, "Hey, did you use the toothpaste from that tube on the right side of the sink?" I replied yes, at which point he yelled for all the world to hear, "That's Bengay!"

I've seen similar scenarios play out many times in conference rooms. Most recently, I was witness to one of the most comical. The senior leadership team was having an important discussion about the organization's sagging employee engagement. One leader was "listening" while on her laptop reading and responding to e-mails. The COO shared a couple of graphs that identified changes over the last two years. The distracted leader looked up and said, "That group has been unhappy and complaining for years." She went on to say that she thought new leadership was needed for that area. After a pregnant pause, one of her colleagues said, "And those are your areas." Having misread the graph while running on autopilot, she experienced her "Bengay moment."

LEARNING

It's always unsettling to see those red and blue lights chasing you down the highway, right? You glance in your rearview mirror and break out in a sweat as you wonder if they're coming for you. You convince yourself they're going after the car in front of you. Not a chance! The police car just pulled up right beside you. You slink lower in your seat, lower that window ever so slowly and say timidly, "Yes, officer?" With a penetrating stare and severe voice, he asks whether you knew you were going eighty in a fifty zone. You, of course, feign ignorance even though you're very aware that you were channeling your inner Mario Andretti. You're so busted! At this point, hope is your only strategy as you wait for the officer and pray that he shows some leniency when writing the ticket. He gives you the ticket, advises you of the particulars and delivers the standard advice: "slow it down." The real kicker is that you go out two weeks later and get another ticket in almost the same spot. This is definitely a learning moment! Now is the time to think about what you can do differently (besides the obvious) to ensure this pattern won't be repeated.

✳ Titter time: Learning ✳

"The difference between stupidity and genius is that genius has its limits."
—Albert Einstein

Self-Help

Feedback exercises

Part 1: Think about your team and the performance of its individual members. Identify a top performer. Reflect on this person's performance and write down what they do well. Don't generalize. Be specific. Determine if this is an objective or a subjective measure of performance (i.e., is their performance based on your opinion or on an objective measure?).

_____

_____

_____

_____

_____

_____

Once you're clear and specific, write them a note (yes, write it by hand, perhaps on nice stationery) about your observations. If this is subjective feedback, use words such as "I believe," "I think" or "I feel." If it's objective, refer to the standard or specific procedure. Share your observations and ask them to keep up the good work and do more of that. Thank them for their contributions.

Part 2: Identify a performer in the middle of the pack who's struggling with an important and objective skill or competence. Define this skill and your observations. Also identify something they do well. Write them a note describing your observations. Be specific. Ask them to reflect on and do more of the positive thing. Offer them a specific tool, training program or mentor to help them with their area of struggle. Thank them for their efforts and let them know you're invested in helping them be successful.

_____

_____

_____

_____

_____

_____

_____

_____

_____

_____

_____

12

It's Time To Reset: Courageously Move From Survive To Thrive

There once was a CEO, a horrible CEO, and he led what his staff fondly called the "island of misfit leaders." While his promotion and title had caused his responsibility and ego to grow, a series of tragic occurrences in his life had also caused his anger to grow. He was a screamer and a thrower of objects (whatever was in reach), and he sought to malign his team in public. He once told me, in an attempt to quiet my disdain for his actions, that this would help his team build character. One morning, as I walked toward his office (as usual, full of dread at the thought of what would greet me), a heavy crystal-like award came sailing down the hall and narrowly missed my face. After the initial shock wore off, I felt thankful that my reflexes had served me well. In the ensuing moments I realized that the projectile's intended target was one of the CEO's other leaders. She was standing there in disbelief, probably wondering if her mind was deceiving her or if someone had truly just thrown a heavy object at her. The CEO realized he'd missed his target and was upset with the leader because she'd ducked and his precious award had broken. And we were both in trouble for not ensuring its safety. This was the final straw! The constant fear of what the next day would bring had taken a toll. Time to make a change and get away from this environment. I went back to my office and began composing my resignation letter—that alone felt quite liberating. Lucky for me, a few other horrific events occurred (in a matter of hours) that led to this CEO's dismissal before I delivered my letter. Crisis averted. It was time to take a few deep breaths and move toward a reset.

The L3 Fusion Model: A journey to transformation

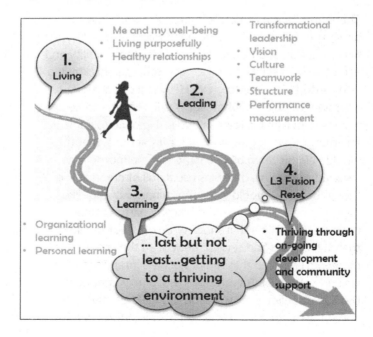

As we prepared to write this book, we interviewed many female organizational leaders from multiple industries and at various levels of leadership across the country. Our goal was to hear their voices—their struggles and triumphs, concerns and dreams—so that we could focus our content on what was important to them. (By the way, we talked to male leaders as well and heard many of the same stories and concerns). We spent time with leaders in the workplace and in interviews from the frontline to the boardroom. Their input was invaluable, and we're honored and humbled that they took the time to share their stories with us. We thank them.

Voices of leadership

Three common themes emerged from our structured interviews with female leaders:

- They experience a sense of guilt and/or anxiety regarding balancing personal and professional needs

- They lack the confidence and willingness to act in the midst of "stupid"

- They have a need to connect to people they can trust to help them along the way

The L3 Fusion Model addresses each of these themes throughout the book and in summary below.

Balancing personal and professional needs— mission impossible?

It's too easy to let our health (physical, mental, emotional, spiritual) go as we focus on meeting everyone else's needs, but this is counter to healthy living and leading. Many women actively participate in others' development. While this is important and fulfilling, it too often comes at the cost of our own health. It's important to put on our own oxygen mask first, so to speak, before helping others—even our children. Without oxygen, we cannot think clearly or be our best selves.

The L3 Fusion Model begins with a call to become healthier. Central to healthy living are healthy habits. These habits enhance our self-esteem, strengthen our bodies and improve our self-image. But healthy living is more than this. It also involves discovering and living out of our inner truth, or purpose— that force inside us that brings energy, vitality and meaning to our lives; that force that builds on our passions, strengths and desires and is hitched to a cause greater than ourselves (Pink 2011). When we live purposefully, we live with intention. We make choices daily that drive our time, conversations, resources and decisions in ways that expand our purpose rather than contract it. We live more purposefully when we routinely check in with ourselves and make choices and set boundaries that keep us aligned with our inner truth. Living purposefully gives us focus and direction and promotes balance in our life: #LivePurposefully.

Healthy relationships are also central to our health. Several attributes and/or contributors to healthy relationships are included in this model—the ability to understand and manage our genuine thoughts, feelings and tendencies better, the ability to connect and empathize with others and treat them with courtesy and respect in spite of our differences, and the ability to give and take in relationships as we strive for win-win scenarios. Psychologists tell us that when we have at least one person with whom we can be emotionally honest, we're much more apt to be mentally healthy. Healthy relationships don't just happen, though. They require an investment of our time, energy and self. The L3 Fusion Model suggests practical ways to build healthy relationships personally and professionally: #BuildYourROR.

Self-confidence and a willingness to act

We found many leaders who were committed to their jobs in spite of overwhelming stress as a result of work overload, conflicts, role ambiguity, organizational constraints and ambiguous priorities. When over-whelmed, many leaders chose to stay under the radar rather than make waves to achieve their personal and organizational goals. As a result, they became increasingly disengaged from the work with growing feelings of anxiety, apathy and / or depression.

The L3 Fusion Model is designed to build leaders' self-confidence through the development of a new mindset that sees the organization differently. It provides a clear view of organizational life through seven lenses—vision, culture, teamwork, leadership, structure, performance measurement and learning. The model provides key principles and tools to support new ways of leading and build competence over time. We identify the "stupid" and provide evidence-based recommendations to stop it in real and practical ways.

The strength of the L3 Fusion Model is that it's an integrated approach based on science. It emphasizes that there is no cut-and-dried approach to leadership. Leading in dynamic times is messy work that requires some trial and error. This mindset of experimentation and integration, along with key principles and tools, gives leaders confidence, as they struggle through the complexity of the systems in which they work— confidence to ask questions, challenge old assumptions, propose and try new ways of doing business, and make mistakes, learn from them, get back up and keep going. The key principles are summarized in the following table.

Summary of Key Principles for Healthy Organizational Leadership

Organizational lens	Principle	Hashtag
Transformational leadership	Leaders push leadership downward and create the conditions for the members to effectively problem solve, make good decisions and do their best work.	#LeadersPrepareTheWay
Vision	Vision is clear and compelling and guides the daily work.	#OhThePlacesWeCanGo
Culture	The culture is action oriented with a transcendent culture that trumps professional and team norms. The collective behaviors promote healthy relationships, diversity and dialogue.	#ElevateYourCulture
Teamwork	Teams are inclusive, action oriented and accountable for results.	#SuitUpForTheTeam

Organizational lens	Principle	Hashtag
Structure	Structures are compatible with culture and facilitate the flow of information horizontally and vertically to enhance effective problem solving and decision making.	#ChannelTheEnergy
Performance measurement	Measures link local goals to organizational goals, are as close to real time as possible, and are meaningful and impactful.	#BeCarefulWhatYouMeasure
Learning	Learning systems are in place that promote ongoing learning and the science of performance improvement. Individuals own their own learning.	#OwnYourOwnLearning

The need for connection

Support is needed as we encounter adversity throughout our leadership journey. This adversity may be personal and/or organizational—such as rapid change,
performance or production pressures, increasing
demands, conflicting priorities and ineffective leadership from others. Support makes us resilient, and
when we're resilient, we can bounce back or recover
from negative events. We can absorb the strain and
continue.

As we look at the past and future from new perspectives, formalizing these new ways of living and leading requires connections that will help strengthen us.
Healthy relationships positively influence our sense of
self-worth and self-confidence. They can help us refocus on what's important and provide a steady hand in
times of uncertainty. Organizational resilience is also
achieved through relationships and human processes.
When we foster respectful interactions between members, and when members are aware of how their work
fits into the bigger picture, the members' resiliency is
strengthened along with the organization's (Sutcliffe
2011).

The L3 Fusion Model proposes that we each create
a network of trusted thought leaders and friends to
help us along the way. In redefining leadership and
our role within an organization, we make profound
changes in the way we think and act. The path isn't

always clear. We will make mistakes. At times we may lose our way. But when we have connections in and out of the organization with people who can help us get back up, we become stronger.

Learning to unlearn and relearn

Real learning is slow and often frustrating. But it's essential. We've worked hard to get to where we are today in our organizations, and we're well equipped for the outdated model—but less well equipped for the new. It's like falling several versions behind in our everyday software because we don't want to go through the nightmare of a learning curve. When we finally decide to bite the bullet, we find so many fundamental changes and new features that we decide to put the upgrade on pause. We go through the stages of change (the same as the stages of grief)—denial, anger, bargaining, depression and finally acceptance that we'll have to invest the time and energy into learning a new way. We start the process and go through these stages again as we learn, unlearn and relearn.

The same is true when it comes to learning new ways of living and leading. We struggle to accept and adapt our leadership even in the face of sound evidence and warnings of danger. The denial stage is perpetuated by impediments within our own mind and within our organizations. Several of the more common impediments and their antidotes are described below.

- Too much noise—All the noise and nonessential data in the workplace makes it difficult to hear and communicate the essential messages. Structures that support respectful dialogue and information-sharing are critical to minimizing the noise.

- Faulty assumptions—We hold onto familiar practices when they're supported by our assumptions. Giving them up requires exposing these faulty assumptions to new evidence and practices. This can be difficult, particularly when they're considered to be evidence of failure. Through respectful dialogue, new evidence and new experiences, faulty assumptions can be exposed and replaced.

- Non-compelling justification—To change deeply entrenched traditions in the workplace, a compelling justification is needed. When this justification (the why behind the what) is clearly communicated and understood, people are more likely to engage in the process.

- Lack of trust—We persist with the old activities when we lack trust in the person telling us to change or when we don't feel safe speaking up, such as in cultures of avoidance and blame. Trust is an outcome of healthy relationships.

- Consequences not understood—We don't change our ways if we believe that doing so won't make much difference or that the social cost will be too high. Often the cumulative effects of small changes don't feel significant (e.g., the fabled frog that boiled to death because it didn't jump out of the gradually heated pot). Consequences are better understood when we can see how our choices and actions are linked to the outcomes.

- Identity crisis—Our daily work behaviors and practices are central to our role as leaders and therefore to our identity. The more educated and/or socially high-profile leaders among us may find it even more difficult to change these behaviors. Changing our identity from a specific role, title or expertise to one of a novice transformative leader can be threatening. An ongoing support system is needed to help us build our resilience and make the needed changes.

Many choose to stay in a state of denial at the cost of effective results. Physicist David Bohm (Bohm 1990, p. 193) eloquently describes this denial state:

> "We are like actors who forget we are playing a role.
> We become trapped in the theater of our thoughts.
> Reality may change but the theater continues.
> We operate in the theater, defining problems,
> Taking actions—losing touch with the larger
> Reality from which the theater is generated."

So how do we move out of our denial state? We'll be more successful when we have colleagues to join us on our journey. It's time to hit the reset button.

It's time for a reset

"I'm the only one who can hit the reset button because this process starts with me." When we're honest with ourselves, we have to admit that we're a bundle of paradoxes:

- I believe there's a better way to lead, and I doubt it

- I want to lead differently, and I like the comfort of my routine

- I feel bad about feeling good

- I feel good about feeling bad

- I want to empower others, and I like control

- I want to learn new skills, and I don't want to admit I need new skills

- I love my title, and I hate my job

- I want to be respectful, and I get satisfaction from talking shit about others

Welcome to the human race. Many of the stupid things we've shared are stupid things we've done or experienced. To create healthier lives for ourselves and those we work with, we can start with understanding and owning our inadequacies, neediness, powerlessness and self-centeredness.

The L3 Fusion reset process begins with understanding and acceptance and quickly moves to planning and action. Just as we created a balanced scorecard for our organizations in Chapter 10, now we must develop a personal reset plan. The goal of this process is to strengthen ourselves and our leadership capabilities through new learning and actions that move us toward a desired future. It's meant to challenge and stimulate critical thinking and drive positive and intentional change. It requires that we be willing to step out of our comfort zone, try new approaches and be open to feedback—#TheL3FusionReset starts with personal introspection.

Let's begin! Work through these statements as you develop your plan.

1. Define your ideal self, the person you want to be. Look through the lenses of your values, behaviors, passions, skills and talents.

2. Define your real self, the person you really are. Look through the same lenses you looked through to define your ideal self.

3. Identify your strengths. These are the values, behaviors, passions, skills and talents that are aligned in #1 and #2 above.

4. Identify your gaps. These are the values, behaviors, passions, skills and talents that are different in #1 and #2 above.

5. Create a statement of your inner truth, your purpose statement, describing who you aspire to be as if you've already achieved this. Here are some starters to get you thinking: "I'm a person who strives each day to . . ."; "I'm committed to being . . ."; "I'm a creative person and an innovator who's willing to . . ."; "I live my life as if . . ."; "I'm committed to being the best . . ."; "I choose to create better conditions for . . ."

6. Develop an L3 Fusion Reset Plan that builds on #3 and reduces #4 for you personally and professionally, moving you toward your inner truth at home and at work. More specifically:

a. Create your inner truth/purpose statement. Write it down. It's a starting point and it can change over time. It's important to getting this process started, so don't worry about semantics or perfection. Get going.

b. You don't have to go full monty on your starter plan. There are five perspectives to consider—healthy me, healthy relationships, healthy leadership, healthy organizations and healthy learning. What's important is to identify one goal and related key action(s) to focus on for two or three of the perspectives. Start small and build on it. Identify meaningful goals that you believe are achievable within the next ninety days.

c. Remember, this is an integrated plan, meaning it's not just about one perspective. It's about all five. It's therefore important to strengthen yourself in each of these areas over time. After the first thirty days, add another perspective and goal. Keep going. If you fall down, get up.

d. Share your plan with someone you trust— someone you can be honest with and who will be empathetically honest in return; someone you believe has your best interests at heart. Set up check-in times every couple of weeks (preferably someplace enjoyable). Mutually commit to making the check-ins a priority.

e. Track your progress. Update your plan. Keep a journal. Celebrate any and all improvements, learnings and achievements.

L3 Fusion Reset Plan

My purpose statement: _____

_____

Perspective	Goal	Measure	Key Actions / Initiatives	Target Date
1) Healthy me a) Finding my inner truth or purpose b) Managing my choices c) Managing my boundaries d) Developing healthy habits e) Other				
2) Healthy relationships a) Managing my relationship(s) b) Setting boundaries c) Developing my negotiation skills d) Building a supportive network e) Other				
3) Healthy leadership a) Setting clear direction b) Driving responsibility downward c) Promoting choice (in the what, who, how, when) d) Improving communication and information flow e) Setting boundaries f) Other				

Perspective	Goal	Measure	Key Actions / Initiatives	Target Date
4) Healthy organizations				
a) Creating and sharing a vision for my area of responsibility				
b) Promoting an action-oriented culture				
c) Promoting diversity				
d) Managing conflict				
e) Loosening and/or tightening controls				
f) Measuring progress and outcomes				
g) Giving and receiving feedback				
h) Other				
5) Healthy Learning				
a) Learning more about systems thinking & methodologies				
b) Using evidence to support change efforts				
c) Seeking additional education/certification				
d) Joining a professional forum or special interest group				
e) Other				

Join our movement

The gap between what organizations need today and what we find in reality is the reason behind the research and writing of this book. One individual can positively impact their area of influence. And when we're joined by others who share that desire, we can eventually tip the scale. Let's together create a movement for healthy living, leading and learning that engages others along the way. Most of us spend thirty-two to sixty hours at work every week. Imagine one hour of well-being improvement multiplied by the number of hours you work per week multiplied by the number of lives you touch. Now that's transformational!

We invite you to join us and the L3 Fusion Movement on our website and participate in a broader community of support and learning. Invite a friend. Take advantage of our many offerings—podcasts, blogs, case studies, coaching and mentoring services, workshops, consulting services and speaking engagements—whatever interests you. We're fun people, and we'd like to have fun with you! Join us at www.L3Fusion.com.

Keeping it real

Your authors are constantly coaching and encouraging others to step out of their comfort zones and try something new (as evidenced in what you've just read).

So when it came time to take our book from an "idea over dinner" to "let's do this," we had a few moments of our own reluctance. We were in unchartered territory, and that sense of doubt was something new for all of us. Did we have something worthwhile to say (together we could be fierce—separate we were boring)? Could we pull this off when we lived hundreds of miles from each other (oh yeah—technology could be our enabler if we kept our time zones straight)? Would we have the will to stick with the book even when it seemed like we might not get to the finish line (someone would need to channel their inner Cruella when necessary). Our response was a resounding "hell yeah!"

Our first workshop together, we committed to holding each other accountable for our deliverables, to challenging ideas respectfully and, most importantly, to being honest with each other about everything—no issue was too small. We needed this book to reflect our personalities without diluting the key messages. There were a few bumps along the way that resulted in us stepping back and identifying our purpose to ensure we could see this to completion. The process could be quite uncomfortable, but we knew we had the courage to face the difficult truths and work through them— together. The strength of the team is what carried us through this process, and we grew to be better leaders as a result.

⋆ *Titter time: Getting started* ⋆

"I did a pushup today. Well, actually, I fell down. But I had to use my arms to get back up, so . . . you know, close enough. I need some chocolate."
   —Unknown

 ## Self-Help

Create your own L3 Fusion Reset Plan. Share it with someone you trust and who will check in with you regularly (every couple of weeks in the beginning) while you do something pleasant—like drink lattes, sip your favorite adult beverages, sit poolside with no kids, walk leisurely through the park or listen to music. Make it something you look forward to. Track your progress. Celebrate any time you achieve a milestone or have a new insight. And keep us informed of your progress—we are your community and will support you along your journey.

Appendix
Hashtag definitions

1. #StupidGoneViral—Stupid is continuing to think, act and behave in ways that haven't gotten us the results we need, personally and/or professionally. We keep doing these things thinking that if we do them harder or softer or faster the results will be different. Recognize the pattern and stop. The world has changed dramatically. This means we need to change our paradigm of living, leading and learning to something that actually works.

2. #It'sAllAboutMe—Leadership starts and ends with you. It's easy to blame others when things don't go as planned and it's tempting to try to micromanage those around us to get the results we want. But the reality is that the only behavior you can truly change is your own. When you

change, others will as well. Leadership, therefore, is first about how you manage your thoughts, emotions and actions in your personal life and your professional life.

3. #LivePurposefully—Purposeful living is intentional, not reactive. It means choosing to do things daily based on our inner sense of rightness, wholeness and truth. This truth is the fusion of our values, beliefs, passions and strengths in our core. This truth brings us energy. When we live purposefully, our lives are less chaotic and more meaningful.

4. #BuildYourROR—No one should go it alone. We all need encouraging, supportive and enriching relationships in our lives. But they don't happen on their own. We create our relationships through our interactions over time. When we interact in thoughtful, healthy ways, we create a strong return on our relationship (ROR) that brings sustenance and resilience.

5. #LeadersPrepareTheWay—Leaders create the conditions for others to do their work—the work of effective decision-making, problem-solving and action. They prepare the way through multiple small actions throughout the day, such as setting the tone, connecting the work to the vision, promoting dialogue and exchange of ideas and providing the necessary information, tools and resources. Small actions can make a big difference.

6. #OhThePlacesWeCanGo—When people understand where they're going, they can help the organization get there, even without a detailed map. Leaders help their teams understand how their work connects to the greater purpose, or destination, giving meaning to their work. This creates a movement that's organic and steady, rather than forced and difficult.

7. #ElevateYourCulture—Cultures can be defined and understood. And cultures can be anywhere from deadly to magical, so they shouldn't be ignored. Leaders have the power to perpetuate or change the culture in their area of influence. To change a culture you must understand the underlying beliefs and expectations that drive the current behaviors and address them one by one.

8. #SuitUpForTheTeam—In organizational life we spend much of our time on teams, and so often, this is time wasted. But teamwork is critical in today's organizations. Whether we're the team leader or a member, we need to be prepared and suit up for this work, not sit on the sidelines.

9. #ChannelTheEnergy—In today's dynamic organizations, we need more than formal, top-down management reporting relationships. When greater specialization and expertise are required, structures will leverage the energy—information, knowledge and experience—of all the members. Through horizontal structures, leadership is distributed to all levels of the organization, up,

down and across, to the people or teams with the right insight and expertise.

10. #BeCarefulWhatYouMeasure—Measurement drives performance. Performance measurements, when designed well, are a critical management tool to keep us on track. They help communicate the strategic objectives, provide direction and inform our activities and decisions. When designed poorly, they can distort the truth and take us down the wrong path, getting us into trouble.

11. #OwnYourOwnLearning—Fundamental to our personal and professional success is a commitment to lifelong learning. This commitment requires investing in healthy learning practices that enhance our awareness of the dissonance between our current thinking and new information around us.

12. #TheL3FusionReset—This is a personal-development process for leaders who want to move from their current state to that of transformational leader. The goal of this process is to strengthen ourselves personally and professionally through new learning and actions that move us toward a desired future. The process challenges and stimulates critical thinking and drives positive and intentional change. It requires that we be willing to step out of our comfort zone, try new approaches and be open to feedback. Individuals are supported through connections with others, including their L3 Fusion team.

Bibliography

Ancona, D., Backman, E. & Isaacs, K. (2019, July–August) "Nimble Leadership: Walking the Line Between Creativity and Chaos." *Harvard Business Review*, 74–83.

Bennet, A. & Bennet, D. (2004) *Organizational Survival in the New World: The Intelligent Complex Adaptive System.* Oxford: Elsevier Butterworth-Heinemann.

Bohm, D. (1990) *Unfolding Meaning.* New York: Routledge & Kegan Paul Inc.

Bolman, L. & Deal, T. (2013) *Reframing Organizations, 5th ed.* San Francisco, CA: Jossey-Bass.

Buckingham, M. (2009) *Find Your Strongest Life: What the Happiest and Most Successful Women Do Differently.* Nashville, TN: Thomas Nelson.

Buckingham, M. & Goodall, A. (2019, March–April) "The Feedback Fallacy." *Harvard Business Review*, 92–101.

Capra, F. (2002) *The Hidden Connections: Integrating the Biological, Cognitive and Social Dimensions of Life Into a Science of Sustainability.* New York: Doubleday, NY, pp 41-42.

Casciaro, T., Edmondson, A. & Jang, S. (May–June, 2019) "Cross-Silo Leadership: How to Create More Value by Connecting Experts from Inside and Outside the Organization." *Harvard Business Review*, 130–139.

Collins, J. (2009) *How the Mighty Fall: And Why Some Companies Never Give In.* New York: Harper Collins.

Collins, J. (2001) *Good to Great: Why Some Companies Make the Leap . . . and Others Don't.* New York: Harper Collins.

Dixon, N. (1999) *The Organizational Learning Cycle: How We Can Learn Collectively, 2nd ed.* Cambridge: Cambridge University Press.

Dörner, D. (1996) *The Logic of Failure: Recognizing and Avoiding Error in Complex Situations*. New York: Metropolitan Books.

Fink L. (2019) Chairman letter to CEO-Investor Relations—BlackRock. Accessed August 21, 2019 at www.blackrock.com/corporate/investor-relations/larry-fink-ceo-letter.

Fisher, R. & Ury, W. with Patton, B. (ed.) (2011) *Getting to Yes: Negotiating Agreement Without Giving In*. London: Penguin Books.

Goleman, D. (1998) *Working with Emotional Intelligence*. New York: Bantam Books.

Goleman, D., Boyatzis, R. & McKee, K. (2002) *Primal Leadership: Realizing the Power of Emotional Intelligence*. Boston, MA: Harvard Business School.

Griffith, S. (2019) *Flipping the Iceberg—The Hidden Science of Reliability in Our Everyday Lives*. Unpublished manuscript.

Gulati, R. (2019, July–August) "The Soul of a Start-Up: Companies Can Sustain Their Entrepreneurial Energy Even as They Grow." *Harvard Business Review*, 84–91.

Hazard, G., Jr. (1996) "Conflicts of Interest in the Classic Professions," in Spece, R.G., Shimm, D.S. & Buchanan A. (eds) *Conflicts of Interest in Clinical Practice and Research*. New York: Oxford University Press, 85–104.

Healy & Serafeim (2019, July–August) "How to Scandal-Proof Your Company: A Rigorous Compliance System Is Not Enough." *Harvard Business Review*, 42–59.

Herman, J. (1997) *Trauma and Recovery*. New York: Basic Books.

Johnson, S., Christfort, V. & Christfort, K. (2017, March–April) "Pioneers, Drivers, Integrators and Guardians." *Harvard Business Review*, 49–56.

Kaplan, R. & Norton, D. (2001) *The Strategy-Focused Organization*. Boston, MA: Harvard Business School.

Kaplan, R. & Norton, D. (1996) *The Balanced Scorecard*. Boston, MA: Harvard Business School.

McElroy, M. (2003) *The New Knowledge Management: Complexity, Learning, and Sustainable Innovation*. Burlington, MA: Elsevier.

Morlinghaus, C. (2019, July–August) "Digital Doesn't Have to be Disruptive: The Best Results Can Come from Adaptation Rather Than Reinvention." *Harvard Business Review*, 95–103.

Pink, D. (2011) *Drive: The Surprising Truth About What Motivates Us.* New York: Riverhead Books.

Plagnol, A. & Easterlin R. (2008, December) "Aspirations, Attainments, and Satisfaction: Life Cycle Differences Between American Women and Men." *Journal of Happiness Studies,* 9(4), 601–19.

Poole, M. (2004) "Central Issues in the Study of Change and Innovation," in Poole, M. & Van de Ven, A. (eds.) *Handbook of Organizational Change and Innovation.* New York: Oxford University Press, 3–31.

Rothkopf, D. (2008) *Superclass: The Global Power Elite and the World They Are Making.* New York: Farrar, Straus and Giroux.

Safar, J., Defields, C., Fulop, A., Dowd, M. & Zavod, M. (2006) "Meeting Business Goals and Managing Office Bandwidth: A Predictive Model for Organizational Change." *Journal of Change Management,* 6(1), 87–98.

Scott, K. & Pringle, J. (2018, January–March) "The Power of the Frame: Systems Transformations Framework for Health Care Leaders." *Nursing Administration Quarterly,* 41(4).

Scott, K. & Mensik, J. (2010, August) "Creating the Conditions for Breakthrough Clinical Performance." *Nurse Leader,* 8(4), 48–52.

Scott, K. & Steinbinder, A. (2009, July) "Innovation Cycle for Small- and Large-Scale Change." *Nursing Administration Quarterly,* 33(4), 335–341.

Senge, P. (1990) *The Fifth Discipline: The Art and Practice of the Learning Organization.* New York: Doubleday.

Sutcliffe, K. (2011) "High Reliability Organizations (HROs)." *Best Practice & Research Clinical Anaesthesiology,* 25(2), 133–144.

Weick, K., & Sutcliffe, K. (2001) *Managing the Unexpected: Assuring High Performance in an Age of Complexity.* San Francisco, CA: Jossey-Bass.

Wheatley, M. (2017) *Who Do We Choose to Be? Facing Reality, Claiming Leadership, Restoring Sanity.* Oakland, CA: Barrett-Koehler.

Acknowledgments

A special thank you to our spouses: Daniel Scott, James Sarikas and Steven Bessler. We thank you for your continuous encouragement and unrelenting support regardless of our quest or course. You have our love and gratitude always. A special thanks to our children: Josh, Jon and Jake Docusen; Kent, Greg and Kathy Scott (yes, there are two!); Amy Carter; Abigail Sarikas; Stephanie, Matthew and Steven Bessler (yes, another one!); for keeping us relevant, humored and always in learning mode. You feel more like dear friends as your thoughtfulness and encouragement have been inspiring through the years. We thank the many members of our extended families for their ability to keep us grounded and comforted when the roads we chose may have been a bit bumpy. You all have made our journey fun, challenging and full of hope for the future. It is our next generation that keep this journey of healthy living, leading and learning at top of mind as we strive for a better world with them.

We are so grateful to our friends, business partners and colleagues who provided us valuable advice, brainstorming and editing sessions of the manuscript and an abundance of laughable and memorable moments. We would not have taken this journey without your encouragement and support. But most importantly we thank you for your friendship: Robert Tarola, Christine Brown-Quinn, Greg Conderacci and Dr. Kathy Malloch.

Our deepest gratitude to The Honorable Kathleen M. O'Malley. We thank you for the time you gave us in getting to know you and for reading and commenting on our manuscript. You are an inspiration to many and certainly to these authors.

We thank the many individuals we interviewed as part of our research and who shared with us their personal journeys around living, learning and leading. Without your openness and honesty this book would not have been possible. We promised confidentiality but you know who you are, and you have our heartfelt thanks.

Thank you to Lucy McCarraher, Eve Makepeace, Rachel Small, Anke Ueberberg, Joe Gregory, Roger Waltham and the entire team from Rethink Press for believing in us enough to publish this book. You have our sincere thanks for editing our words and unwavering support of this book.

The Authors

Kathy A. Scott, PhD, MPA, BSN, RN
Partner and Co-Founder, L3 Fusion LLC

Kathy A. Scott is President and Chief Executive Officer of a firm she established in 2010 in Phoenix, Arizona. Her name-sake firm specializes in healthcare working with executives and teams to transform traditional leadership, clinical and business models to alternatives that will thrive in a highly competitive environment. Dr. Scott holds a PhD in Healthcare Administration and Organizational Systems, a master's degree in Public Healthcare Administration and a bachelor's degree in Nursing; and is a former long-term Fellow in the American College of Health-care Executives. Her doctoral research served as the science behind "Stupid Gone Viral." Her expertise was gained through multiple chief executive roles (nursing, operations, innovation, integration) in several medium and large healthcare systems. Kathy is a recognized expert in transforming organizations to achieve high reliability structures and processes. She is also a noted speaker and author on contemporary leadership, large-scale organizational change, clinical transformation and patient safety. She does all this with a flair for engaging her audiences with candor and a sense of humor.

Bridget Sarikas
Partner and Co-Founder, L3 Fusion LLC

 Bridget Sarikas is Vice President of Right Advisory LLC, a firm based in Washington, DC that she co-founded in 2008. Right Advisory provides financial improvement services to organizations struggling with the challenges of a changing business environment—particularly US healthcare, US higher education and global multinational organizations. Bridget's contribution to these organizations is that "she stops the stupid." She gets stuff done by using her multifaceted experiences in music, psychology, administration, financial analysis and investor relations. She is an expert in process improvement using

all the modern tools such as six sigma, lean and just-do-it. She is a graduate of Indiana University and has honed her skills over 30+ years in management roles with businesses diverse as global professional services, global chemical manufacturing and US health and education systems. She conducts her work and achieves success through a proper balance of grit and grace - empowering and training others to achieve their potential. And she does this with an unassuming sense of humor that allows for a relaxed work setting focused on meeting goals and expectations.

Christine Bessler
Partner and Co-Founder, L3 Fusion LLC

Christine Bessler is a seasoned expert and executive in information systems and technology. She has provided strategic direction within Information Technology divisions in building effective governance models, establishing Business Intelligence Centers of Competency, Project Management Offices and technology education teams. Her special business and technical skills are in strategic alignment, organizational change leadership, growing new programs to support transformational strategies, business process re-engineering, and needs assessments. She is also a creative talent - and is the artist of our illustrations and website design. Christine is the backbone

251

of our L3 Fusion team developing our "look" and media content. She translates our leadership thesis in everyday management and has developed accredited courses on the topics of change management and portfolio and project management. She is a certified change agent and a retired Project Management Professional (PMP).

⊕ www.L3Fusion.com

Made in the USA
Coppell, TX
12 March 2020